Par écrit

Writing French for GCSE

Ena Fowler

OXFORD UNIVERSITY PRESS 1987

Oxford University Press, Walton Street, Oxford OX2 6DP

Oxford   New York   Toronto
Delhi   Bombay   Calcutta   Madras   Karachi
Petaling Jaya   Singapore   Hong Kong   Tokyo
Nairobi   Dar es Salaam   Cape Town
Melbourne   Auckland

and associated companies in
Beirut   Berlin   Ibadan   Nicosia

Oxford is a trade mark of Oxford University Press

Acknowledgements

The author would like to thank the editors for being so pleasant and
helpful, and her husband, who has helped in many ways.

Illustrations are by Katie Thomas and Chris Wadden.

Cover illustration by Sue Heap.

Photographs are by:

John Brennan p.34; Keith Gibson pp.35 (right), 51, 52, 57; Kate Minogue
p.37; Spectrum Colour Library pp.35 (bottom), 36 (left); Swiss National
Tourist Office p.36 (right); Topham p.35 (left).

The publishers would like to thank the following for permission to
reproduce copyright material, or for providing reference material:

Brasserie Löwenbräu p.53; Chambre de Commerce et d'Industrie de
Boulogne-sur-Mer et de Montreuil p.24; *Dépêche du Midi* p.22; Fédération
Unie des Auberges de Jeunesse pp.43, 46; *Figaro* pp.18, 21; Guide Susse du
Camping p.45/6; Hoverspeed Ltd. pp.29, 31; Ministère des Postes et
Télécommunications p.60; Office Municipal du Tourisme de La Ciotat
p.28; Publications Filipacchi: *Girls* pp.18, 75, 80, *OK! âge tendre* pp.18, 75,
Pariscope p.74, *Podium-Hit* pp.49, 73; Relais du Silence p.47; SNCF French
Railways p.27; Tourisme Équestre du Gers en Gascogne (Maison de
l'Agriculture, Route de Tarbes — BP 99, 32003 Auch cedex p.37; Voyages
Fram p.23.

Although every effort has been made to contact copyright holders, a few
have been impossible to trace. The publishers apologize to anyone whose
copyright has been unwittingly infringed.

Typeset by Tradespools Ltd., Frome, Somerset
Printed in Great Britain by William Clowes Ltd., Beccles

Preface

Par écrit has been written to prepare students for the written section of the French GCSE examination.

For ease of reference, the book takes one by one the topic areas designated by the various examination boards, and gives practice at both basic (general) and higher (extended) levels. The student is guided through the different writing activities required by the new syllabuses, from form-filling, lists, notes, messages, and postcards, to letters and semi-guided narrative. In addition, some French oral practice is suggested (by the symbol 【) as it arises from the written work, or vice versa. The oral work is a higher-level activity in that it is open-ended. However, it is straightforward enough for basic-level students to profit by it also.

Selected English–French vocabulary lists, based on the new syllabus requirements, are given within each section, and there is a general English–French vocabulary at the end of the book.

It is hoped that by working through this book students will obtain a step-by-step, clear, and thorough introduction to all the varied aspects of the new French writing syllabuses.

Key to symbols:

No symbol —	suitable for basic (general) level
▶	suitable for both basic (general) and higher (extended) levels
▶▶	suitable for higher (extended) level only

Notes:
(i) At basic level, pupils are required by most boards to write fewer words. In this book the words 'if you have space' are included in the instructions to allow the pupil to answer the question at either level.
(ii) In order to comply with the requirements of some examination boards, teachers may like to give more specific instructions for the letters.

Contents

Introduction

Hints on writing postcards and letters

1 Decide whether you should use **tu** or **vous**, and don't switch from one to the other. As a general rule, **tu** is used in writing to friends of your own age, and to relations. **Vous** is used when writing friendly letters to older people, and in formal letters such as booking a room at a hotel.

2 Decide whether your letter is formal (written on business, or to a stranger) or informal (between friends). There are certain differences to remember:

	Formal	Informal
vous *or* **tu**	**vous**	**tu** or **vous**
Layout	your full address and date at top right	name of your town only, and the date, at top right
Commercial layout	recipient's name and address underneath your own and above the date	
References and enclosures	on the left, opposite the date	
Beginnings	**(Cher) Monsieur (Chère) Madame**	**(Mon) cher Pierre (Ma) chère Marie Cher ami/chère amie**
Endings	**Veuillez agréer, Monsieur/Madame, l'expression de mes sentiments distingués**	**Bien à toi A bientôt Je t'embrasse Sincères salutations** (to someone older)

3 Make a list of what you think are the dozen most useful verbs in the **tu** and **vous** persons, and learn them, e.g.
Tu dis que (vous dites que) . . . You say that . . .
Tu me demandes si (vous me demandez si) . . . You ask me whether . . .
Veux-tu . . .? (voulez-vous . . .?) Do you want to . . .?

4 You can write a simple but lively letter with the help of exclamations and idioms, such as:

    Quelle chance!   What good luck!
    C'est formidable, ça!   That's marvellous!
    C'est dommage, ça!   That's a pity!

You can make your own list from your reading.

5 If you are replying to a letter, make sure you answer all the questions you are asked. Then, if space allows, show an interest in your friend's affairs by commenting on his/her news and asking questions of your own.

    This needn't be difficult. You can repeat the news, changing the verb, and make a suitable remark, e.g.

    Tu vas aller en Amérique? C'est formidable, ça!

    Then, if you have space, a question or two such as 'When?' 'What do your parents think of it?' would naturally follow.

    Some useful phrases are:
    Qu'est-ce que?   What?
    Quand est-ce que?   When?
    Pourquoi est-ce que?   Why?

General hints

1 Don't write more than the number of words asked for.
2 Your narratives should not be over-ambitious. They can be simple and yet interesting if you put in conversation and idioms, and vary your tenses correctly.
3 Try to use verbs and phrases that you know are correct, and not to translate word-for-word from English.

1 You and your family

Where you live

address une adresse
flat un appartement
floor un étage
lift un ascenseur
postcode le code postal
street la rue
town la ville
village le village

Appearance and character

awful affreux (-euse)
beautiful, handsome beau (belle)
charming charmant
fair blond
fat, big gros (grosse)
funny drôle, amusant
nice sympa(thique), gentil(le)
old âgé, vieux (vieille)
pleasant agréable
polite poli
pretty joli
red (*hair*) roux (rousse)
short court

shy timide
slim mince
stupid stupide
tall grand
thin mince, maigre
ugly laid
young jeune

Greetings and farewells

good afternoon/good morning bonjour
good evening bonsoir
good night bonne nuit
have a good journey bon voyage
have a good weekend bon week-end

good luck! bonne chance!
happy birthday! bon anniversaire!
happy New Year! bonne année!
happy Saint's day/name-day! bonne fête!

see you later à toute à l'heure
see you soon à bientôt
see you tomorrow à demain
see you on Saturday à samedi

1 a Below is a family tree sent to you by your new French
pen-friend. Draw your own family tree in the same
way.

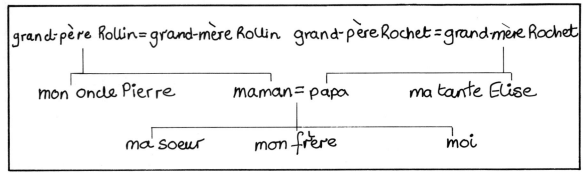

grand-père Rollin = grand-mère Rollin   grand-père Rochet = grand-mère Rochet

mon oncle Pierre   maman = papa   ma tante Elise

ma soeur   mon frère   moi

b For each member of your family tree, write:
   1 what his/her name is
   2 how old s/he is
   3 what town s/he lives in

2 a Describe the people in the pictures below, giving each a name, and saying something about their appearance and character. Write about 15 words for each one.

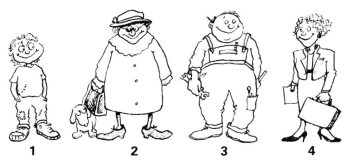

1 **2** **3** **4**

b Describe the appearance and character of the person you admire most—and the one you admire least! Write about 30 words for each description.

3 Imagine you are helping your parents to fill in this booking form for a holiday abroad. Copy it out and fill in details about the members of your family who are going on the holiday.

VILLAGE ARC-EN-CIEL
27/33, QUAI LE GALLO
92517 BOULOGNE CEDEX
Tél.: 604.91.78
(Postes 32.98-35.91)

HIVER 1984/85

BULLETIN D'INSCRIPTION
(à retourner à l'adresse ci-dessus avec votre règlement)

NOM : _____ Prénom : _____ Date de naissance : _____

Adresse complète : _____

_____

Profession : _____ Tél.: Domicile : _____
                                          Bureau   : _____

Régime Sécurité Sociale (général ou autres). Préciser : _____

COMPOSITION DE LA FAMILLE PARTICIPANT AU SEJOUR

NOM et Prénom	*Date de naissance	Lien de parenté	Profession

Nombre total de participants (y compris chef de famille) : _____
Numéro carte d'adhésion de l'année en cours .... : _____
Personnes à prévenir en cas d'accident : _____ Tél.: _____
SEJOUR CHOISI : *(mettre une croix ou les dates (NOEL/JOUR DE L'AN) dans la case correspondante).*

4 Your French friend, who has never seen you, has agreed to meet you at the Gare du Nord, Paris. Write a postcard saying when exactly you will arrive, and how s/he will recognize you.

5 Write a postcard to your French pen-friend, saying that you have recently moved house (**to move house** déménager). Give your new address and add some news or greetings.

6 Write a postcard to your French pen-friend explaining why you haven't written for such a long time. Say you will write a letter soon.

7 Write a postcard to your French pen-friend, saying that you hope s/he is feeling better. Give some news of your family and send their greetings.

▶ **8** Using the first page of the *bulletin d'inscription* as a guide, write a letter to the parents of an imaginary French boy or girl with whom an exchange has been arranged, introducing yourself, and giving as much of the information (in letter form) as you have space for.

BULLETIN D'INSCRIPTION—1

NOM: .... PRÉNOM: ....

SEXE: .... DATE DE NAISSANCE: ....

PROFESSION DU PÈRE: .... PROFESSION DE LA
                                                    MÈRE: ....

COMPOSITION DE LA FAMILLE (âges):

FRÈRES: .... SOEURS: ....

HABITEZ-VOUS		AVEZ-VOUS:	
un appartement	☐	un jardin	☐
une maison	☐	une salle de bains	☐
en ville	☐	une douche	☐
en banlieue	☐	une voiture	☐
à la campagne	☐	la télévision	☐

Le jeune étranger aura-t-il une chambre individuelle?
  OUI/NON

L'enfant sera-t-il emmené en vacances? Où? ....

Votre enfant est-il déjà allé à l'étranger? OUI/NON Quel pays? ....

Quelles distractions pensez-vous offrir au jeune étranger pendant son séjour? ....

9 Using the second page of the *bulletin d'inscription* as a guide, help your mother or father by writing a letter in French describing what you are like, stating your preferences, and giving any advice your parent(s) feel(s) is relevant.

BULLETIN D'INSCRIPTION—2

Votre enfant

Quelles langues étudie-t-il? ....

Depuis combien de temps? ....

Est-il:

tranquille	☐	petit	☐
plein de vie	☐	moyen	☐
timide	☐	grand pour son âge	☐
sociable	☐	méticuleux	☐
réservé	☐	désordonné	☐

Quels sont ses goûts intellectuels? ....

Joue-t-il d'un instrument? ....

Quels sports pratique-t-il? ....

Avez-vous des recommandations spéciales? ....

Autorisez-vous votre enfant à sortir seul?   OUI/NON   Si oui, jusqu'à quelle heure? ....

---

10 Write a first letter to a new French pen-friend, describing yourself and your family and pets. If you have space, state your hobbies, your likes and dislikes, and ask similar questions about your new friend.

11 Write a letter in French to your pen-friend, thanking him/her for the present recently sent to you. Say why you like it.

Give news of yourself and your family. Has anything exciting happened recently?

If you have space, ask questions about your friend and his/her family which refer to their news, e.g. a sister or brother may be getting married or going to university; someone in the family might have started a new job or been made redundant. (**to be made redundant**   être mis au chômage)

12 Write an article for a French teenage magazine after your recent stay in France, describing the differences you have noticed between the French and English ways of life, their buildings, amenities, amusements, food, etc. Say what you have most liked and/or disliked.

2 House and home

The house and its rooms

block of flats un immeuble
building le bâtiment
council flat un HLM
flat un appartement

basement le sous-sol
bathroom la salle de bains
cellar la cave
conversion un aménagement
converted aménagé
entrance une entrée
floor, storey un étage; **floor** (*of room*) le plancher, le parquet **ground floor** le rez-de-chaussée; **on the first/second floor** au premier/deuxième étage
lift un ascenseur
yard la cour

Inside your home

appliance un appareil
armchair le fauteuil
bath la baignoire
blanket la couverture
broken down, not working en panne
bulb une ampoule
cassette recorder le magnétophone (à cassettes)
central heating le chauffage central
channel (*on TV*) la chaîne
contraption le machin
couch, settee, sofa le canapé, le sofa
cupboard le placard

curtain le rideau
dustbin la poubelle
freezer le congélateur
fridge le frigo, le frigidaire
furnished meublé
hi-fi une hi-fi, une chaîne haute-fidélité
hoover, vacuum cleaner un aspirateur
plug, socket la prise (de courant)
radio la radio, le poste (de radio)
saucepan la casserole
sheet le drap
stereo la chaîne-stéréo
switch l'interrupteur
tap le robinet
tape recorder le magnétophone
video recorder le magnétoscope
washing machine la machine-à-laver

Useful verbs

to brush brosser
to clean nettoyer
to clear débarrasser (la table)
to economize ménager
to help donner un coup de main (à)
to hoover (*a room*) passer l'aspirateur (dans une pièce)
to move house déménager
to phone donner un coup de fil
to rent louer
to repair réparer
to sweep balayer
to wash up faire la vaisselle

1 a You are about to buy this studio flat in Paris. Make a list in French of the furniture, linen, and kitchen equipment you would like to buy for it. List ten items, and for each one state either its colour, size, or material, or something else about its appearance.

b With a partner, discuss (preferably in French) the points you would hold in mind when buying a flat or house. Ask questions such as 'Veux-tu un jardin?'
After discussion, each of you can compile your own list in French of ten items.

2 a Here is a plan of a flat you have visited. Make a list of the rooms, with the main furniture in each room, in order to describe it to your French friends. There should be a total of 20 items, including the names of the rooms. List also ten appliances or conveniences it does *not* possess.

You may wish to discuss the question with a friend first, and pool your ideas.

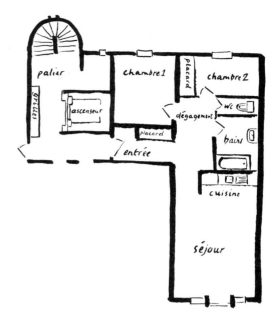

ch. la chambre bedroom
degt. le dégagement passage, open space
grilles *(f)* bars
pl. le placard cupboard
v.o. le vide-ordures rubbish chute

b Write a letter to your French friend describing your holiday in the above flat. Say what you like about it, and describe what you are doing.

3 Here is a competition in a French magazine. Make a list of the items pictured, putting the most important one first. Then complete the tie-breaker.

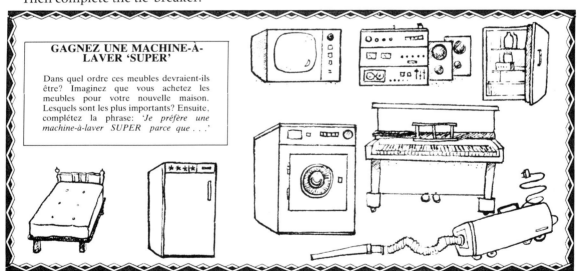

GAGNEZ UNE MACHINE-À-LAVER 'SUPER'

Dans quel ordre ces meubles devraient-ils être? Imaginez que vous achetez les meubles pour votre nouvelle maison. Lesquels sont les plus importants? Ensuite, complétez la phrase: *'Je préfère une machine-à-laver SUPER parce que . . .'*

4 Leave a message in French for the cleaner who is coming to help in your holiday home, listing what s/he should do in the house, e.g. tidy up, clean, do the washing . . .

5 Leave a message in French for the workman who is going to spend a week repairing and cleaning your very old French cottage. List the items of furniture or appliances which are in need of repair. Give brief guidance as to what should be done. Repair? Paint? Clean?

6 Le jeu des différences

a Write down in French the differences between the two pictures below. There are ten differences, not counting this example:

Picture 1   Les carottes sont sur la table.
Picture 2   Les carottes sont dans la casserole.

b Write down in French the ten differences between these two pictures, e.g.

Picture 1   La fenêtre est ouverte.
Picture 2   La fenêtre est fermée.

(**on the floor**   par terre)

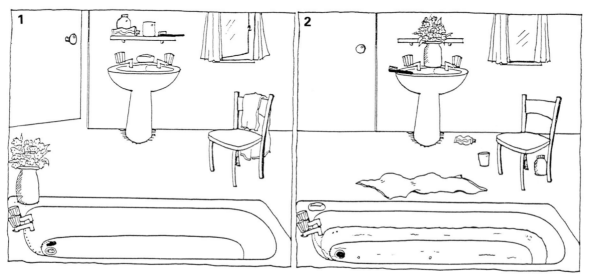

7 You and your French pen-friend have been left to look after the house for a week. Make out a timetable for each of you, sharing out the housework. Each of you has two tasks per day. Don't repeat any phrases exactly. For Saturday and Sunday say how you are going to enjoy yourself after all your hard work!

	lundi	mardi	mercredi	jeudi	Vendredi	Samedi	dimanche
Mon copain / ma copine	1) nettoyer la salle à manger 2)						
Moi	1) allez chez le boucher 2)						

8 You are staying in France for a few months and would like to buy ten items, either for yourself or to take home. Make a list of the items, and against each one write the appropriate price and how you hope to acquire the money for it, e.g. birthday present? housework? shopping? gardening? washing cars? Don't repeat any phrases.

disque	F70	laver quatre voitures

9 a Make out a check list in French of the kind you may receive when renting a 'gîte' in France. Base it on the house plan below; you should list what movable items of furniture and equipment there are in each room, so that the owner can check that nothing is stolen. Omit the small items of kitchen equipment. Write a total of 15 items.

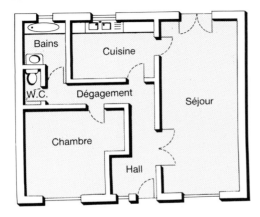

15

b Now make out a check list for the kitchen equipment. The picture below may give you some ideas. Write a total of 15 items.

10 Write about 30 words on the following subject. A friend is about to look at a flat in France which the family may rent, and has asked you for advice. Make a reminder list of what questions the family should ask, under the following headings:

    a bathroom   **c** sitting room
    b kitchen   **d** bedrooms

The questions may be about conveniences (hot water? central heating?) or about appliances (television? etc.). You need not write full sentences.

11 Your French friend, Jean, has sent you this postcard:

> Paris, le 2 Juillet
> Nous passons les vacances chez nous cet été. Tant pis! Je me lève à huit heures, je fais le ménage, j'écoute mes disques. Quelquefois je vais à la piscine. L'après-midi, je fais du sport. Le soir je sors avec mes copains.
> Qu'est-ce que tu fais à présent?
> Bien à toi,
>   Jean

Write a postcard in reply to Jean. Tell him that you are at home too. You get up around nine o'clock. In the afternoon you go for walks and at night you go to a disco or club.

16

12 You have received this postcard from Angélique, who lives in France:

> Lille, le 9 juin
>
> Salut !
> Je t'écris parce que nous avons déménagé. Ma nouvelle adresse est 21, rue des Rois, Lille. C'est un quartier tout neuf. Il n'y a pas beaucoup d'usines ici; il y a un parc, une piscine et un club des jeunes tout près. J'aime beaucoup la nouvelle maison.
> Ecris-moi bientôt,
> Angélique

Write a postcard in French to Angélique, thanking her for her card. Say that she is lucky. Near your house there are lots of factories—and no youth club.

▶ **13** Write a letter to your French pen-friend describing your home. Say whether you live in a house or a flat, and whereabouts it is. Does it have a garden or a garage? How many bedrooms are there? What furniture is there in your bedroom? (Mention at least two items.) What is there on the wall? Say that you like listening to records and watching television.

▶ **14** Read the following letter, then write a reply to Monique in French, answering her questions, and remembering to include the date. For a shorter letter at basic level, limit the number of questions you answer.

> Dear Chris,
>
> Thank you very much for your letter. I'm glad you're going to be my pen-friend.
>
> Please tell me about yourself and where you live. Do you live in the country or in a town? Where's your school and what's it called? What time do you get up, and how do you get to school? Do you have lunch at school? What subjects do you like, and what don't you like? What time do you arrive home? Do you have a lot of homework?
> Best wishes,
> Monique.

15 The following letters appeared in French magazines. Imagine you are the 'agony aunt' and write suitable replies.

a

Lydie X., Tarbes:
« JE NE SUPPORTE PLUS MA FAMILLE… »

J'ai quatorze ans et j'estime que mon problème est beaucoup plus important que ceux des lectrices qui se plaignent de ne pas avoir de flirt ou bien de l'avoir perdu ou encore d'avoir un petit bouton sur le nez… Aussi, j'espère que vous le retiendrez et me remonterez le moral. Voilà: je ne supporte plus du tout ma famille! Je la trouve nulle, archi-nulle! Mon père ne s'intéresse qu'à sa voiture, au foot et au Loto. Ma mère ne parle que de «son» ménage, de «sa» vaisselle, des voisins qui ont fait ci ou dit ça quand elle ne me reproche pas ma façon de m'habiller ou de me maquiller (légèrement pourtant), les copines et les copains que je fréquente, etc. Il y a des moments où je préférerais, finalement, être orpheline…

b

Martine 15 ans

«Ma sœur est une dragueuse»

Chère Geneviève,
Ma sœur est une dragueuse. Elle fume, elle fait « sa craneuse » son intéressante. Je ne peux plus la supporter. Elle se maquille pour être plus belle que moi, c'est insupportable. Comment lui faire arrêter cela ?

c

Martine X., Nantes :
« JE NE SAIS RIEN DE LUI »

Je sors avec Gérald depuis deux semaines. Nous nous entendons parfaitement mais il y a quelque chose qui m'intrigue chez lui : dès que je lui pose des questions sur ses parents, l'endroit où il habite, qui il fréquentait avant de me connaitre, etc., il devient muet. Pourtant, lui, sait tout de moi (ou presque). Me cache-t-il quelque chose ?

16 Imagine that you are an estate agent trying to sell a flat or house in the rue Victor-Hugo to parents of young children. Describe the amenities of the area with reference to the map below.

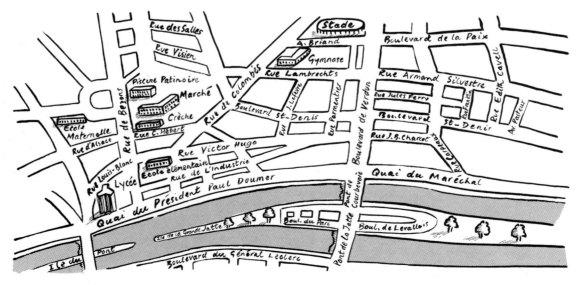

17 Read the following letter, then write a reply to Robert in French.

> Samedi, le 4 Mars
>
> Ma chère Paulette,
>
> Merci bien de ta lettre. Je t'écris très tard — il est minuit — j'ai été très affairé aujourd'hui car tous les samedis je travaille dans un garage près de chez nous. Je gagne 20 francs par heure.
>
> J'arrive au garage à huit heures, et d'abord je nettoie la salle d'exposition. Puis je lave les vitres des autos, et ensuite je vends de l'essence. Quelquefois j'aide à réparer les pneus — j'aime ça. Qu'est-ce que tu fais le samedi ? Est-ce que tu as un emploi ?
>
> Bien à toi,
>
> Robert.

18 Here are some notes made by a policeman who arrived at the scene of a burglary.

Write a full account of this burglary just as you think the policeman would do on returning to the police station. If you like, include some conversation with the owner of the house.

> arrivée — 10 heures
> cuisine — feu
> salle à manger — téléviseur volé
> salon — argenterie disparue
> chambres — en désordre.

argenterie silverware

19 Send a letter to your pen-friend saying that you are working hard because your mother and father have 'flu. Tell your friend what you are doing in the house to help. Ask how s/he is and what s/he is doing.

3 Weather and places

What's the weather like?

clear clair
cloudy nuageux (-euse)
cool frais (fraîche)
dismal, dull triste, maussade
freezing glacial, givrant
hot chaud
mild doux (-ce)
misty brumeux (-euse)
overcast couvert
poor mauvais
rainy, wet pluvieux (-euse)
snowy neigeux (-euse)
stormy orageux (-euse)
sunny ensoleillé
variable variable

When?

yesterday hier
today aujourd'hui
tomorrow demain
the day after tomorrow après-demain

Where's the wind?

au nord

N

à l'ouest **W** ← → **E** à l'est

S

au sud

Types of weather

bright interval une éclaircie
cloud le nuage
drizzle la bruine
fog le brouillard
ice la glace; **black ice** le verglas
mist la brume
rain la pluie
shower une averse
snow la neige
storm un orage, une tempête

1 a Draw the symbols which appear at the foot of the map at the top of p.21, and write against them what they stand for, in French and English.

▶▶ **b** Read the weather forecast given beside the map, and write down the English for the following words:

nuageux	orienté
brumeux	le verglas
matinal	un brouillard
une averse	givrant
un temps couvert	en moyenne montagne
le littoral	vraisemblable
se désagréger	une éclaircie
un déclenchement	atteindre

c Imagine you are a French news reporter. Make up a short weather forecast by referring to the map and symbols, and answering these questions in French:

Dans quelle partie de la France les vents seront-ils
    faibles?   forts?
    modérés?   orageux?

En France aujourd'hui

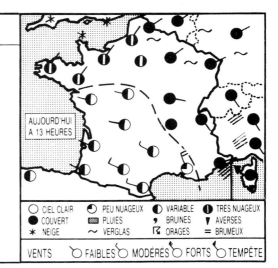

RÉGION PARISIENNE. – La journée restera nuageuse et localement brumeuse. Les températures matinales seront voisines de 0° ou faiblement négatives, et les maximales approcheront 3 à 4°.

AILLEURS. – Le matin des averses se produiront sur la Corse et un temps couvert affectera le littoral méditerranéen (pluie et neige dans les Alpes). Les nuages se désagrégeront dans la journée avec déclenchement temporaire d'un vent de secteur nord-ouest. Températures minimales de 5 à 7°.

Des régions littorales de la Manche au Nord et au Nord-Est, temps couvert avec des vents qui restent orientés au secteur est. Températures minimales de – 3 à – 6°, quelques chutes de neige possibles et, en tout cas, formation de verglas.

Sur les autres régions, le temps restera nuageux et des brouillards localement givrants se formeront. Températures minimales de 0 à – 2°.

En soirée, de la Bretagne à l'Aquitaine, le temps se couvrira, donnant des pluies et, en moyenne montagne (Pyrénées, Massif central), de la neige. Températures maximales atteignant 7 à 8°.

Sur le Nord, le Nord-Est et l'Est, maintien vraisemblable d'une bonne couverture nuageuse. Températures maximales encore basses : 0 à – 2°. Ailleurs, quelques rares éclaircies se développeront et les températures pourront atteindre 2 à 4°.

Dans quelle partie de la France y aura-t-il
de la neige? un ciel un peu
un temps couvert? nuageux?
un temps variable? des pluies?
du verglas?

2 a Write an account in French of the weather in France from this map. Say where it is snowing/cloudy/overcast, and say where the wind is weak/moderate.

b Correct the following statements about the map:

1 Le temps sera généralement ensoleillé sur toutes les régions du nord.
2 Le temps sera généralement chaud dans les régions du nord-est.
3 Les vents seront faibles dans les régions du nord-ouest.
4 Il va faire très chaud dans le midi.
5 Dans les régions littorales de l'ouest, le temps sera nuageux.

c You are staying on the Mediterranean coast of France near the Spanish border, and the weather is as shown on the map. Write a postcard to your French friend. Include two statements about the weather, and say how you are passing the time.

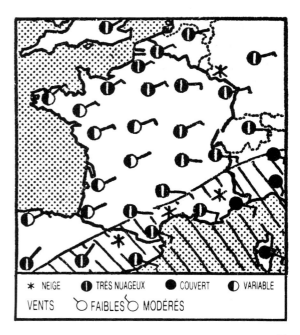

21

3 Write out the following weather report in full,
substituting the correct terms for the pictures:

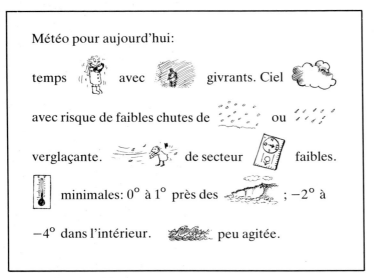

coasts   les côtes (*f*)

4 a Draw the symbols which appear at the
sides of the map on the right, and write
against them what they stand for, in
French and English.

▶▶ **b** Read the weather forecast given below
the map, and write down the English for
the following words:

brumes matinales	rafales
aggravation	éclaircies
orages	grains
grêle	occidentale
vent d'autan	niveaux

c Your French friend must have been
dreaming when s/he prepared these
weather notes for you from the map. Can
you correct them?

Bordeaux : averses   Le Puy :
ensoleillé Biarritz : vent faible
Lourdes : vent fort Perpignan :
temps couvert Narbonne : brume
Montpellier : neige Nîmes :
averses Cahors : ensoleillé
Périgueux : brouillard

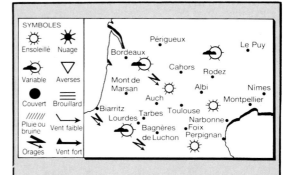

MIDI TOULOUSAIN ET REGIONS LIMITROPHES

Quelques brumes matinales. Beau temps chaud
durant la journée. Aggravation dans la soirée
avec développements d'orages pouvant être
accompagnés de grêle. Vents faibles puis
modérés de sud-est. Vent d'autan parfois assez
fort. Rafales de sud-ouest sous orages.

Températures minimales entre 16 et 18
degrés, maximales entre 27 et 30 degrés.

PYRENEES CENTRALES ET OCCIDENTALES

Après de larges éclaircies, évolution orageuse
avec grains débutant sur la partie occidentale de
la chaîne. Orages localement forts avec grêle et
rafales largement positives de secteur sud-
ouest. Températures restant largement
positives à tous niveaux.

La Dépêche du Midi

5 Correct the following statements about the map below:
1 Grau Roig est au nord de Bonascre le Saquet.
2 Andorre-la-Vieille est à l'est des Escalades.
3 Prades est au sud d'Ax-les-Thermes.
4 Pas de la Case est à l'ouest des Escaldes.
5 Canillo est au nord-est de Soldeu.

Now make up five correct statements of your own.

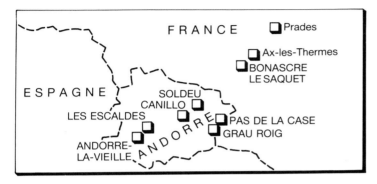

6 Your pen-friend is thinking of visiting you soon. Make him/her a list in French of your town's amenities, e.g. features of historical interest, places of natural beauty, interesting buildings, and facilities for shopping and amusement. Write about 30 words.

▶ **7** Imagine that you live in St Cyprien, which is shown in this plan. You read a letter in a magazine criticizing the place as a holiday resort. Write a reply to the magazine saying why you think it is a great place for a holiday.

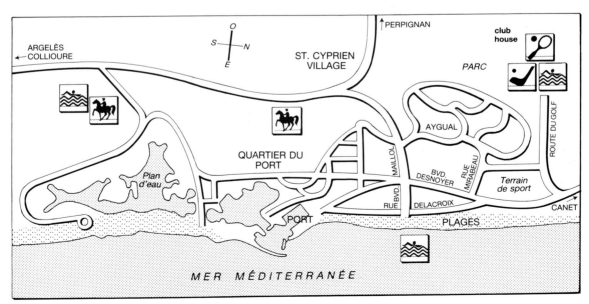

8 You have just spent a weekend in Paris. Make a brief diary of your stay (about 30 words altogether), stating for each day what the weather was like and where you went. Don't repeat yourself, e.g.

    vendredi
    chaud
    matin—visité le marché
    après-midi—bateau mouche sur la Seine
    soir—disco

9 a Using the map below, make notes for yourself and your French friend on the activities you plan for a day in Boulogne. For example, say where you hope to go and what you intend to do or buy. Write about 30 words, e.g.

    syndicat d'initiative—demander une carte et des brochures

b You have to leave directions in French for a friend who is meeting you. Using the map below, tell your friend
  1 how to get to the cathedral from the station.
  2 how to reach the swimming pool from the cathedral.
  3 how to get to the post office from the swimming pool.

c While you are in Boulogne write a postcard in French to your pen-friend in Lille. Say what the weather is like and what you are doing.

▶ **d** Write a longer letter to another French friend after you are home again, describing in detail where you went and by what transport. If you have space, describe the sights you saw, and anything interesting or amusing which happened.

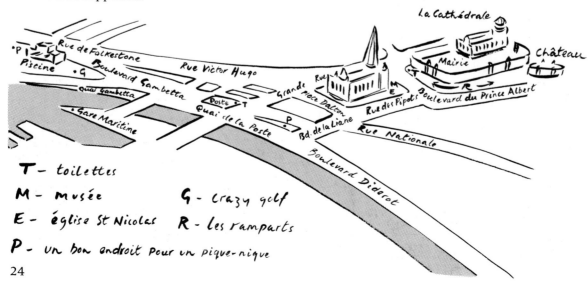

T – toilettes
M – musée   **G** – crazy golf
E – église St Nicolas   **R** – les ramparts
P – un bon endroit pour un pique-nique

10 Write a tourist brochure entry for the area shown in the map below. Give the names and routes of the main roads, describe where the castles and citadels are, and make two other comments on the landscape or sights.

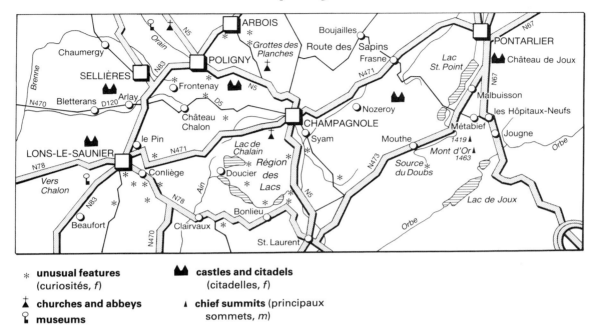

* **unusual features** (curiosités, *f*)

▲ **churches and abbeys**
♀ **museums**

▲▲ **castles and citadels** (citadelles, *f*)

▲ **chief summits** (principaux sommets, *m*)

11 Your French pen-friend has written to you saying that s/he will be visiting a town not far from you in the summer, with a school party, and s/he would like to visit you. Write a letter welcoming him/her and arranging to meet him/her. If you have space, suggest a few places of interest you might visit together.

12 Write an account of a day spent in Boulogne using the pictures below. Describe in detail where you went, by what transport, the sights you saw, and anything amusing or interesting which happened.

4 Travel and transport

At the booking office

booking, reservation   la réservation
counter, ticket office   le guichet
information   les renseignements (*m*)
price   le prix
reduction   la réduction
return (ticket)   un aller-retour
single (ticket)   un aller simple
ticket   le billet (*rail*); le ticket (*bus, tube*)
timetable   un horaire
tourist information bureau   le syndicat
   d'initiative (S.I.), le bureau de tourisme

Methods of travel

by air   en avion
by boat   en bateau, par le bateau
by bus   en bus, en autobus, avec le bus
by coach   en car, en autocar
by ferry   en ferry
by metro   en métro
by motorbike   à moto, à vélomoteur
by scooter   en scooter
by taxi   en taxi
by train   en train, par le train

Going by car

boot   le coffre
to **break down**   être (tomber) en panne
crossroads   le carrefour
diversion   la déviation
driving licence   le permis de conduire
engine   le moteur
insurance certificate   la carte d'assurance
make (*of car*)   le marque
map   la carte;   **road map**   la carte routière
to **park**   stationner
parking   le stationnement

Going by train

arrival   une arrivée
class   la classe
compartment   le compartiment
corner   le coin
couchette   la couchette
customs   la douane
delay   le retard
departure   le départ
to **deposit**   déposer
entrance   une entrée
excess fare   le supplément
exit   la sortie
line   la ligne, la voie
left-luggage locker   la consigne automatique
luggage   les bagages (*m*)
occupied, taken (*of seat*)   occupé
platform   le quai, la voie (*each 'quai' has two
   'voies'*)
to **punch (ticket)**   composter
railway   le chemin de fer;   **French
   Railways**   la SNCF
reserved   réservé
to **smoke**   fumer;   **(no-) smoking**   (non-)
   fumeur
train   le train;   **fast train**   un express;   **non-
   stop or through train**   un train direct;
   express train   un rapide;   **stopping train**
   un omnibus

Useful phrases

forbidden   défendu, interdit;   **. . . is
   forbidden**   défense de . . ., il est défendu
   (interdit) de . . .
free   libre, gratuit
from   de;   **originating from**   en
   provenance de
to **hitch-hike**   faire de l'autostop
in advance   en avance

1 You are alone in the house of your pen-friend Alain
   Dubois. You answer several phone calls and make rough
   notes (opposite). Now write these messages up in French,
   so that the family can understand them. Write 20-30
   words for each message.

1/ Solange phoned from Villepinte. She has puncture + will arrive at 8 p.m.

2/ Pierre phoned. When will Alain arrive at station tomorrow? They want to pick him up. Please call back.

3/ Mme Charpentier rang. She's sorry – can't meet Mme Dubois on Thursday at station. Mme D. must take bus no. 57.

4/ Henri phoned. Motorbike has broken down so he'll have to spend night in Rheims. Will arrive tomorrow afternoon.

2 a Complete this account of Amélie's arrival at the Gare du Nord in Paris. Fill in the gaps by referring to the numbers and the key. Add a beginning and an ending to the letter.

Je suis arrivée dans la cour des Arrivées à midi exactement. Je suis allée à **1** pour envoyer une carte postale à Pierre, ensuite à **5** car j'avais trop de bagages. Tout près j'ai trouvé **6** pour dire bonjour à maman. J'ai cherché **3** pour voir s'il y avait un restaurant à la gare, mais – pas de chance! Ensuite j'ai trouvé un petit enfant égaré qui pleurait; je l'ai donc amené à **19**. Il fallait acheter **4**, car j'habite à Chantilly. J'avais très faim – je suis donc sortie de la gare près du **15** et j'ai traversé la rue. Dans la rue St-Quentin j'ai trouvé un joli petit bistro, où j'ai déjeuné. A deux heures je suis retournée à la gare, j'ai repris mes valises de **5** et je suis montée dans le train pour Chantilly.

Automatic Luggage Lockers (5) (17) (22)		Post Office (1)	
Car Park (14) (15)		Taxis (10)	
Information (9)		Telephone (6)	
Left Luggage (16)		Tickets (Paris suburbs) (4) (7) (11)	
Metro (8) (13) (21)		Toilets (2)	
Plan of Station (3) (20)		'Tourisme SNCF'- (travel agency) (18)	
Police Station (19)		Train timetables (12)	

b Help Amélie by putting the key into French.

3 a You are writing a French brochure for visitors to La Ciotat. Prepare the instructions you would write for a tourist's walk around the town, starting from the lighthouse (**le phare**) near the town hall, and going past the following places:

1 the market near the post office
2 the square J. Jaurès
3 the Eden theatre
4 the museum

With a partner, you can practise giving directions orally. One of you is a local resident and the other is a visitor who asks directions. Remember to swap roles.

b Write a letter to a French friend from La Ciotat. You have just spent an enjoyable fortnight's holiday there, and want to recommend the resort to your friend. Look at the map and find a few points of interest. Tell your friend why it would be fun to visit these places. The weather there was good, so if you have space, include two or three things you did on the beach.

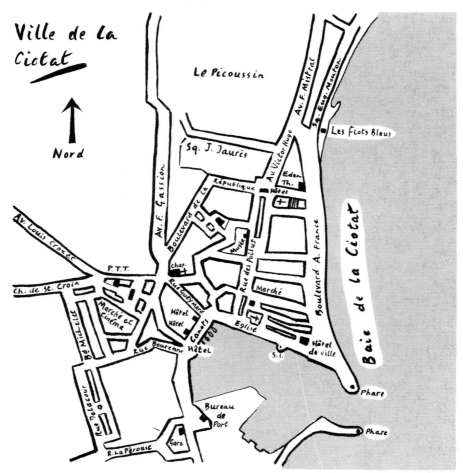

Ville de La Ciotat

Nord

28

4 You want to phone your pen-friend in Paris with some information about a journey you are going to make there. Using the timetable below, make notes in French to prepare for the phone call.

LONDON to PARIS

28 October to 30 April (except 25 December)

PERIOD OF OPERATION		A	DAILY	B	DAILY	C	B	DAILY	D	E	F
London Victoria	dep.	—	08 04	—	10a 30	—	—	14a 15	—	20 55	20a 45
London Charing Cross	dep.	07 45	—	09 55	—	10 55	12 55	—	15 55	—	—
London Waterloo (East)	dep.	07 47	—	09 57	—	10 57	12 57	—	15 57	—	—
SEA CROSSING		🚢	⛴	🚢	⛴	🚢	🚢	🚢	🚢	⛴	⛴
Paris St-Lazare	arr.	—	18 07	—	—	—	—	—	—	07 02	—
Paris Nord	arr.	14 37	—	16 32	18 23	17 40	19 30	22 28	23 02	—	09 13

These timetables only show departure and arrival times. In some cases it may be necessary to change trains en route. Full details can be found in the British Rail International Passenger Timetable, price £1 and available from principal British Rail stations and newsagents.

🚢 — Sealink Ship   ⛴ — Hoverspeed Hovercraft

A Daily until 4 November, 21 December to 2 January (except 25, 26 December), 15 to 24 February and from 29 March; also Fridays and Sundays 1 to 24 March.
B Daily (except 25, 26 December).
C Mondays, Fridays and Sundays from 1 April; also 30 March, 4, 19, 13 April, 16, 28 May.
D 31 March, 4 to 9, 12 to 15, 19, 21 April.
E 4 April only.
F Daily (except 24, 25 December).
G Daily from 31 March (except 7 April, 26 May).
H 8 April only.
a Mondays to Fridays dep. 15 minutes later.
b Fridays dep. 1704
    Sundays to Thursdays dep. 1707
*Arrivals in London on Saturdays and Sundays may be up to 19 minutes later than shown owing to Engineering works.

It would be a good idea to get used to the timetable first by practising, either orally with a partner, or in writing. Here is the pattern to follow when asking the questions:
   C'est le . . . (date). On part de . . . (station) à . . . (time). On arrive à . . . (station) à quelle heure?

You have four possible departure times in mind. For each of them tell your friend:
1 whether the crossing takes place daily or at certain limited times
2 whether the crossing is by ship or hovercraft
3 at what station and time you will arrive in Paris

The suggested departure times are:
   London Victoria 08.04
   London Charing Cross 09.55
   London Waterloo 10.57
   London Victoria 20.55

5 Write a reply to the postcard below, saying that you can't go to Waterloo station to meet your friend on that day as you have an exam, but your mother will go. If you have space, say that you are looking forward to the visit of your friend.

J'arrive à Londres (Waterloo) le 18 juillet à 18.00.
Est-ce que tu peux venir à ma rencontre?

6 You are about to phone a French travel agency, but decide it would be wise to make notes first on what you want to say. You wish to book a 2nd class student single ticket from Paris to London, travelling tomorrow morning by train and ferry. You would like to know how much it will cost, and ask if there are any no-smoking compartments.

This is how your request would look in table form:

Ticket	Destination	Travel by	Date	Other questions
single 2nd class student	London	train and ferry	tomorrow	

Make notes on what you would have to say.

Now make notes for the following bookings. You can also practise orally with a partner, making sure you swap roles.

Ticket	Destination	Travel by	Date	▶▶ Other questions
return 2nd class adult	Dover	train and hovercraft	16 June	Is it a non-stop train? What time does it arrive at Dover?
single 1st class adult	Marseille	air	17 July	Can you buy perfume on the plane? How long is the flight?
single 2nd class student	Berlin	coach	18 Aug.	Where is the coach station? What time does the coach leave Paris?
return tourist class student	Geneva	air	next month	Which airport is the flight from? What time does it land in Geneva?

7 Write a letter to a French travel agency enquiring about a rail journey you wish to make. Say where you are going and where you want to leave from. Do you want a single or return ticket? Second or first class? Ask how much the journey will cost, and ask them to send you a timetable.

8 You have just spend a week-end with some friends in Paris. Write a postcard saying you have arrived home safely, and thanking them for their hospitality.

30

9 a Write a letter based on this booking to your pen-friend, who is to meet you in Paris. Give the place and time of arrival and the coach and seat numbers. You have never met before, so if you have space, describe yourself and say that you enclose a photo.

b Write a postcard such as your French friend might write in reply, saying that s/he will meet you at the station. If you have space, write some extra news.

10 a Write a letter to the Paris branch of CitySprint booking two single student places from Paris to London on the coach which leaves Paris at 11.00 on 15 January (name the flight). Say that you enclose a photocopy of each student card. If you have space, ask what time the coach arrives at Calais, say that you enclose a cheque for the amount required (work out from the leaflet what it is), and ask another question or two, such as what happens if the weather is bad – is there a flight just the same?

b The reason you wanted to know what time the coach arrived at Calais in question 10a is that you are meeting your pen-friend there, who is coming with you to England. Write a letter to your pen-friend, saying what time you are reaching Calais, and asking him/her to reserve a flight on the same hovercraft. If you have space, say that you will be pleased to see him/her, and mention what you plan to do during his/her stay in England.

c Write a letter to a friend in Paris, telling him/her that you will be travelling with your brother and sister (aged 3 and 12) on the coach which leaves London at 11.00 on 1 February (name the flight). Ask your friend to meet you where the bus stops (arrowed on the map) and tell him/her what time it will arrive. If you have space, say how you plan to entertain your brother and sister while in Paris.

Seat Reservations Ticket Garde-Place Sitzplatz Reserviering	TRANSALPINO B.I.G.E. Mr/Mrs/Miss J. FOWLER.					
	Sections Parcours Strecke	Train Zug	Date Tell	Time Heure Uhr	Coach Voiture Wagen	Seat Place Platz
From de von to a nach	LONDON VICTORIA FOLKESTONE		18 APR.	14.00	A	7B.
From de von to a nach	CALAIS – PARIS NORD	H.OO.	18 APR.	19.30.	33.	17.

HOVER*SPEED*

horaires & tarifs
PARIS – LONDRES
CALAIS – LONDRES

CITY*SPRINT*

du 1er NOVEMBRE au 28 FEVRIER

PARIS - Rue de St-Quentin - Métro : Gare du Nord
LONDRES WC1 – Royal National Hotel – Bedford way
Métro : Russell Square

HORAIRES	DEP. PARIS	DEP. CAL.	ARR. LON.	ARR. DOV.	DEP. LON.	DEP. DOV.	ARR. CAL.	ARR. PARIS
1/11/84 au 28/02/85 sauf 25.12.84	EN HEURES LOCALES							
Vol 631	11.00	16.30	16.05	18.50				
Vol 631					11.00	14.00	15.35	20.10

TARIFS aller simple	ADULTES	jeunes * + 14 / - 18	enfants + 4 / - 14	moins de 4 ans
PARIS - LONDRES	240 F	230 F	185 F	GRATUIT
PARIS - DOUVRES	215 F	205 F	165 F	GRATUIT
CALAIS - LONDRES	210 F	195 F	165 F	GRATUIT

* TARIF APPLICABLE AUX ETUDIANTS (sur présentation de carte)

Hoverspeed, 24 Rue de Saint-Quentin, 75010 Paris. Téléphone : 260.36.48. Près de la Gare du Nord.

▶ **11 a** You have received the following letter:

> Cher Christopher,
>   J'attends avec impatience ma visite en Angleterre. Je serai très content de te revoir. Je compte arriver le mercredi 20 août à Victoria. Peux-tu venir me chercher à Victoria (le train arrive à 14.30)?
>
>   A bientôt,
>   Jean-Paul.

Write a reply, saying that you are extremely sorry, but you cannot meet Jean-Paul at Victoria. (Put the date on your letter.) Explain to him what number bus to catch outside Victoria and where to get off. Give instructions for the short walk he must then make to reach your house.

   If you have space, say why you can't meet him at Victoria, but assure him that he is very welcome.

b Follow up this letter with a phone call to Jean-Paul. Make notes in French for the call, in which you are to:

   ask if he has received the letter
   tell him you can meet him at the station after all
   explain that your neighbour has a car and will
      come with you to the station
   confirm the meeting times
   tell him that you are looking forward to seeing
      him.

▶▶ **12** Write an account, based on the pictures, of a journey from Paris back to England.

5 Holidays

abroad   à l'étranger
camera   un appareil (-photo)
country   le pays
countryside   la campagne
dating from   à partir de
fortnight   quinze jours
guide   le guide
holidays   les vacances (*f*);   **summer
  holidays**   les grandes vacances
hotel   un hôtel
journey   le voyage
sea   la mer;   **at the seaside**   au bord de la mer
tourist   le touriste

tourist office   le bureau
  de tourisme
travel agency   une agence de voyages
trip   une excursion
week   la semaine
weekend   le weekend

to be on holiday   être en vacances
to go camping   faire du camping
to set off on holiday   partir en vacances
to spend (*time*)   passer
to stay, remain   rester
to sunbathe   se faire bronzer

1 You are in France, planning a camping holiday with your
French friend. Make out a list in French of items you may
need. Write about 20 words.

2 Imagine you work as a customs officer in France. What
would you say were the probable contents of these four
travellers' bags? List five different items for each person.

3 These teenagers are planning their holiday. Make a list in French of what you think they may be hoping to do. Write about 30 words.

4 You have arranged to spend a few days' holiday in Paris with your French friend. When you arrive at the hotel you had chosen, you find that it is booked up. Leave a message for your friend saying that the hotel is full, that you are looking for another hotel, and that you will meet him/her in the foyer at 6 p.m.

5 You have arrived first at the hotel where you are going to spend your holiday with a French friend. You witness an accident and have to go to the police station. Leave a message for your friend, giving this news and saying you don't know what time you will be back.

6 a Make up a large magazine advertisement to describe the attractions of the resort below.

▶ **b** Write a letter based on the photograph to your French friend, saying where you are, when you arrived, and who is with you. If you have space, describe what you plan to do.

7 Write a postcard in French to your pen-friend stating when you will arrive at a certain railway station in France. Ask your friend to meet you there. Arrange where in the station to meet.

8 Here is a postcard sent to you by your pen-friend. Send a postcard in French in reply. Say that you are not having a very nice time as it rains often. You are spending the time watching TV and playing cards. Sometimes you play table tennis.

> le 12 juillet
>
> Cher ami,
> Je m'amuse follement ici — temps superbe — je fais des randonnées à cheval et à pied — le soir, il y a des discos superbes
> Écris-moi bientôt,
> Paul

9 Imagine you are staying at one of the places pictured in the postcards below. Write one to your French pen-friend. Describe the place, and say how you are spending the time.

10 Write a postcard in French from the holiday home pictured here. Say what you particularly like about the house or flat. What amenities is it near? How many rooms does it have? What is the view like?

11 a Here is a postcard written by a French boy holidaying in the area shown in picture 1. Write a similar postcard in French, as though you were taking a holiday in the area of picture 2. Alter the underlined words and phrases to suit this picture. The date is 31 December. Say that you are in Switzerland. It's cold and you ski every day. In the evening you spend the time talking to your friends and dancing. You go to bed late, because you are having a good time.

le 8 Août

Nous voici dans le Midi de la France en plein été ! Il fait très chaud. On s'amuse bien – tous les jours, je fais une randonnée à cheval. C'est sensass ! Le soir je passe le temps en mangeant et en jouant aux cartes. Je me couche tôt, car je suis fatigué.

Écris-moi bientôt,

Pierre.

1

2

b Complete the grid with words describing the two pictures. Mention the season, the weather, the amenities, and what you guess to be the animal and plant life.

	Picture 1	Picture 2
Saison Climat Passe-temps Curiosités Plantes Animaux		

▶ c Write a thank-you letter to the French friends who gave you a holiday at one of the above resorts. Say what you particularly enjoyed. If you have space, recall some interesting person or event there, and say that you hope to see your friends next year.

▶ 12 Here is a page torn from a diary. In French, write a letter to a friend, basing it on the diary entry.

mardi 3 Juillet

Toujours en vacances à Cannes. Jour ensoleillé. Matin – les courses – souvenirs et cadeaux – Après-midi – la mer. Magnifique ! Soir – feu d'artifice.

13 a You are writing the descriptions for a French brochure of holiday homes. Write about 30 words on each of the pictures below. For picture 1 describe the landscape and the amenities of the area; for picture 2 describe the whole flat.

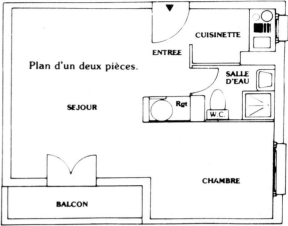

▶ b Write a postcard or letter to your French friend from one of these apartments, describing your holiday.

▶▶ 14 Imagine that you went on a riding holiday to Auch. Using the map below to give you ideas, describe what you did each day. Describe where you went, what you saw, and anything unusual that happened.

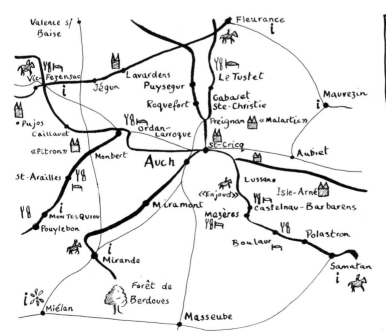

15 Write a letter in French in reply to the following.

> *jeudi, le 21 mai*
>
> Cher Ben,
> J'espère que tu es toujours d'accord pour venir chez moi à Clermont-Ferrand en juillet. Nous irons nous promener en montagne. Si tu veux, nous pourrons faire une excursion de 3 ou 4 jours dans le parc des Volcans et faire du camping. Nous irons nous baigner dans les lacs. Nous ferons de la planche à voile. Je veux te faire visiter le plus possible l'Auvergne. J'espère que tu aimeras ma région.
> L'année prochaine, je découvrirai à mon tour l'Angleterre, grâce à toi.
> Philippe.

16 Write an account in French of a holiday you spent at Saint-Cyprien, based on a few events chosen from the programme shown below. Say who was with you and what you thought of the event. Did any interesting incident happen? Did you meet anyone?

Aide Mémoire du VACANCIER

SAINT-CYPRIEN PLAGE
— ville d'art —

Programme
Festivités de Juillet

TOUS LES MARDIS ET VENDREDIS
Visite touristique gratuite de la station
Renseignements au Bureau du Syndicat d'Initiative

LUNDI 14 JUILLET : Fête Nationale. Cérémonies officielles. A 17 h 00 et 21 h 00, Place Maillol, à la Plage : **BAL POPULAIRE.**
Au Village, à 17 h 00 et 21 h 00 : **BAL POPULAIRE.**
Soirée animée par les Orchestres C. ROLLAND et RETROSPECTIVE.

MARDI 15 JUILLET : Eglise de Saint-Cyprien-Plage : Festival de Musique avec l'ensemble vocal **DUFAY.**
Théâtre de la Mer :
  GALA MICHEL SARDOU

MERCREDI 16 JUILLET : Aux Arènes : **TOROS PISCINE.**

JEUDI 17 JUILLET : Quartier du Port - Place de Marbre, de 18 h 00 à 19 h 30 : **APERITIF FOLKLORIQUE RONDELLA MARIBEL avec les BALLETS POPULAIRES de CATALOGNE.**
Place Maillol, 21 h 00 : Podium Variétés **BASTIEN.**

VENDREDI 18 JUILLET : 14 h 30 : **TOURNOI DE FOOT A 5** au Gymnase de la Plage.
20 h 30 : Carrefour Maillol (rue Dr-Schweitzer) : Spectacle de variétés **M. CLAVERI** et jeux organisés par les **VINS COTES DU ROUSSILLON.**

SAMEDI 19 JUILLET : Aux Arènes : **TOROS PISCINE.**
Au Village : **CONCOURS DE PETANQUE.**
Saint-Cyprien-Village, Place publique : **BAL POPULAIRE.**

▶ 17 Write a reply to this letter.

Dimanche 31 Août

Chère Sarah,

Je viens de rentrer du Sud-Ouest de la France où j'ai passé une semaine avec mes parents et ma sœur Sandrine. Nous étions dans le département appelé le Lot.

Nous avons quitté Paris vendredi dernier. Nous avons pris le train jusqu'à Cahors. Là, nous avons logé dans un petit hôtel très sympathique.

Nous avons visité beaucoup de musées, le Pont Valentré. C'était très chouette ! Nous sommes aussi allés visiter des grottes. Il y a beaucoup de grottes dans le Lot. Le Gouffre de Padirac est très célèbre. Nous avons pris une barque pour le visiter. C'était très impressionnant !

J'ai beaucoup aimé la nourriture et surtout le vin rouge ! Un soir, j'avais bu trop de vin à table (il était si bon !) et maman n'était pas contente. Papa lui a dit que c'était exceptionnel car on était en vacances !

Les soirs, nous allions nous promener le long de la rivière. Nous sommes allés à un bal. Tous les gens dansaient et chantaient. J'ai rencontré Isabelle. Elle a 16 ans et elle habite Toulouse. Elle va m'écrire.

J'ai passé de très bonnes vacances.
Et toi, qu'as-tu fait ? Écris-moi vite.
Grosses bises   Cathy.

6 Accommodation

In a hotel

I'd like to book a room
Je voudrais réserver
  une chambre

What is the cost of a room
Quel est le prix d'une chambre

for one	pour une personne
for two	pour deux personnes
for a family	pour une famille
with one bed	avec un lit
with a shower	avec douche
with a bathroom	avec salle de bains
with a toilet	avec WC

At what time do you serve breakfast/lunch/dinner?
A quelle heure est-ce qu'on | prend le petit déjeuner?
déjeune?
dine?

At a youth hostel or campsite

I'd like to
Je voudrais

Can I
Est-ce que je peux

book a bed   réserver un lit
hire sheets   louer des draps
hire blankets   louer des couvertures
hire a sleeping bag   louer un sac de couchage
hire a site for . . .   louer un emplacement
  pour . . .

General

Our party consists of two adults and three children.
Nous sommes deux adultes et trois enfants.

How far away is | **the beach?**   La plage | est à quelle
the railway station?   La gare | distance?
the town centre?   Le centre-
  ville

At what time do you | **open?**   On ouvre | à quelle heure?
close?   On ferme

How much is it

per day?		par jour?
per person?		par personne?
per night?		par nuit?
weekly?	C'est combien	par semaine?
for half-board?		pour une demi-pension?
		pour une pension
for full board?		complète?

Would you	reply as soon as possible.	Voudriez-vous	répondre aussitôt que possible.
	confirm the reservation.		confirmer la réservation.
	send me some information.		m'envoyer des renseignements.

I enclose . . .   Prière de trouver ci-joint . . .

At a hostel or campsite

air bed, lilo   le matelas pneumatique
campsite   le camping, le terrain (de camping)
floor, storey   un étage
cooker   la cuisinière
dormitory   le dortoir
drinking water   l'eau potable (*f*)
dustbin   la poubelle
lamp, light, torch   la lampe
plug, socket, power point   la prise
rucksack   le sac à dos
rules, regulations   le règlement
sink   le bac à vaisselle, l'évier (*m*)
shower block   le bloc sanitaire
warden   le gardien
youth hostel   une auberge de jeunesse

At a hotel

basement   le sous-sol
deposit   les arrhes (*f*)
form   la fiche
ground floor   le rez-de-chaussée
lift   un ascenseur
luggage   les bagages (*m*)
payment   le règlement
staircase   un escalier
supplement, extra charge   le supplément
telephone   le téléphone
washbasin   le lavabo

1 Look at the picture for two minutes; then close your book and write down in French as many items as you can remember.

You can do this exercise orally with a partner, who can give you hints about the items you have forgotten, e.g. for a tent: 'C'est grand et c'est en nylon'.

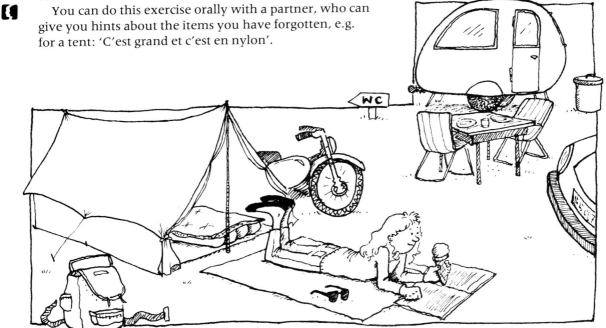

2 Compare the following. For example:
   1 Le sac à dos est plus petit que la valise.

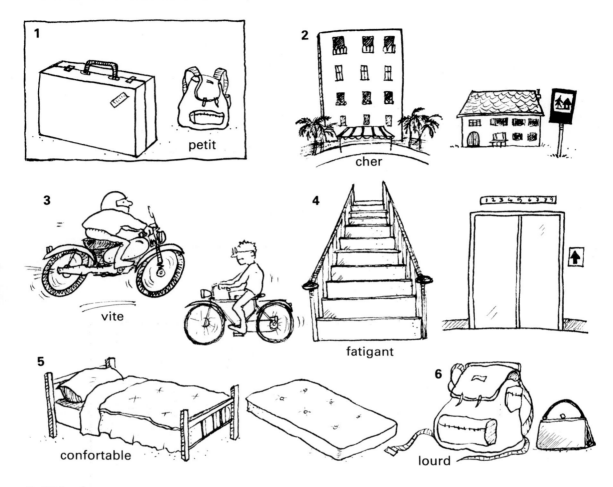

petit

cher

vite

fatigant

confortable

lourd

3 Write down:
   a ten items you would take on a camping holiday.
   b ten different items you would take for a holiday in a hotel.

4 Make a list of:
   a five questions you might need to ask at a campsite.
   b five different questions you might need to ask at a hotel.

You can do this exercise orally with a partner. Take turns at playing the role of the camp warden or hotel manager who answers the questions.

5 Write a postcard to your French friend from a French youth hostel, saying where you are, how you are enjoying your stay, and what you are doing.

6 Replace the pictures with words in the following letter:

Monsieur,

Je vous remercie beaucoup de [picture] de votre [picture] que vous m'avez envoyé et des [picture] [picture] que vous avez indiqués. Avez-vous [picture] à partir du [14 AUGUST] jusqu'au [21 AUGUST]? Nous sommes quatre, [picture] et [picture]. Je voudrais [picture] avec [picture] et [picture] s'il vous plaît.

Est-ce qu'il y a [picture] dans les chambres? Est-ce qu'on peut [picture] dans les chambres? Est-ce que [picture] est loin?

Voulez-vous confirmer la réservation s'il vous plaît?

Veuillez agréer, Monsieur, l'expression de mes sentiments distingués.

Jean Duvalier

[16 JUNE]

7 a Above is an application for a membership card for the 'Fédération Unie des Auberges de Jeunesse'. Copy out the part which is outlined in bold and fill it in.

BULLETIN D'ADHESION INDIVIDUELLE *
(à remplir en caractères d'imprimerie)

Désignation	PRIX
Cotisation annuelle	F
Surprime Ski	F
FFCC: vignette camping à apposer sur carte d'A.J. (vignette valable en France seulement)	F
Carnet camping international/FICC (1) Nº (1 vignette internationale/FICC de l'année comprise) (1)	F
FICC: vignette internationale à apposer sur carnet camping international/FICC	F
TOTAL	F

(1) Le Carnet de Camping international et la vignette FICC sont **COMPLEMENTAIRES** à la vignette FFCC de l'année en cours, apposée sur la carte d'A.J. ou la carte camping (individuelle ou familiale)

NOM

PRENOM

ADRESSE (Nº, nom de la rue)

PROFESSION — voir liste des codes ci-dessous — Code

LOCALITÉ, lieudit ou autres indications utiles

DATE DE NAISSANCE — Cocher la case — SEXE F M

CODE POSTAL — Bureau PTT distributeur

LIEU DE NAISSANCE

NATIONALITE 17

▽ COCHER LA CASE CORRESPONDANTE

J'AI MOINS DE ☐ 18 ans ☐ 26 ans

J'AI PLUS DE ☐ 26 ans

J'AI ADHERE L'ANNEE DERNIERE

☐ OUI ☐ NON

Codes - Catégories socio-professionnelles

10 - Etudiants et Elèves de Grandes Ecoles.
11 - Scolaire et Lycéens.
12 - Professeurs.
13 - Instituteurs.
14 - Employés de bureau des secteurs public et privé.
15 - Personnel para-médical et hospitalier.
16 - Ouvriers : contremaître et ouvriers qualifiés et spécialisés des secteurs public et privé, apprentis divers, manoeuvres, marins, mineurs, etc.

17 - Cadres moyens.
18 - Cadres supérieurs.
19 - Artisans, Commerçants.
20 - Agriculteurs.
21 - Sans profession (mères de famille, etc...)
22 - Autres catégories : personnels de service, artistes, militaires, etc...
23 - Chômeurs.

* La carte délivrée est annuelle et internationale.
Elle est strictement personnelle et non transmissible.
Aucun duplicata ne sera délivré en cas de vol, perte, etc...

Fait à... le.................................
Signature de l'adhérent

Signature des Parents
(obligatoire pour les mineurs)

b Write a letter to the headquarters of the F.U.A.J. (at 6, rue Mesnil, 75116 Paris), asking them to send you a membership card (**une carte d'adhérent**). Say that you enclose the application form (**la demande de carte**), a photo, and the annual subscription (**la cotisation annuelle**).

If you have space, ask them to send you their magazine as well. Say that you want to go on holiday to France in two months' time, and that you hope your membership card will arrive in time. Then ask one or two questions of your own.

8 Write letters to these four youth hostels, booking beds and making enquiries according to the instructions below. If you have space, make any other relevant enquiries.

	Les Pèlerins 74400 Chamonix	Domaine de Bellevue Route de Cannes 83600 Fréjus	6 av. des Oiseaux Bois de l'Ancien Séminaire 29000 Quimper	Place du Pontiffroy 57000 Metz
Can I reserve beds for …?	2 girls	1 boy & 1 girl	3 boys	4 girls
Dates	2–9 June	3–4 July	16–20 Aug.	1–15 Oct.
Can I hire …?	sheets	sleeping bags	—	sheets and blankets
Enquiries	cooking facilities	how far is it to the beach?	what time do you close?	hot showers
How much does it cost for …?	1 week	2 days	4 nights	2 weeks

9 a Write a letter to the holiday flats below, booking a studio flat for one week from 15 June. Say that you are enclosing a cheque for the full amount (which you can work out from the details given). Don't forget to include the insurance fee for cancellation.

   If you have space, ask if there is a beach club for children nearby.

Les Bastides du Grand Stade	PRIX PAR LOGEMENT ET PAR SEMAINE				
Arrivée : samedi 18 h Départ : samedi 10 h	23/3-13/4 25/5-15/6 7/9-28/9	13/4-25/5 28/9-2/11	15/6-29/6	29/6-13/7 24/8-7/9	13/7-24/8
Studio 4 personnes	1 000	850	1 550	2 250	2 600
Appt 2 pièces 6 personnes	1 450	1 100	2 000	2 550	3 000
Garantie annulation + assistance ELVIA : ● studio : 80 F/semaine ● 2 pièces : 100 F/semaine.					

   b Now you are there! Write a postcard to a French friend from your flat, saying that you are having a good time and that there are a lot of young people there. Unfortunately you are sunburnt.

10 a Write a letter to the campsite advertised on p.45 booking a site for your caravan for a fortnight. (Give the dates.) Ask how much you have to send as a deposit.

   If you have space, ask a few questions about the site and its amenities. Is there a swimming pool? Restaurant? Shops? How far away is the nearest town?

CAMPING STELLA MARIS

∗ ∗ N N

Plage de Castouillet - **44490 LE CROISIC**

Tél.: (40) 23.03.71 - Ouvert du 1/5 au 15/9

Terrain deux étoiles proposant un confort supérieur à sa catégorie.

+ Séparé de la mer par la route seulement.

b Write a postcard from the campsite to a French friend, saying that it's hot, you go swimming every day, and you hope that your friend is having a good holiday.

▶ **11** Study the information given by the symbols about the four hotels below. Then write in French to one of them, asking to book a room or rooms for a certain date. Ask if your hotel provides some of the amenities which are mentioned in the abbreviations, but for which no symbol appears against the name of the hotel.

LOCALITÉS HOTELS - ADRESSES	RENSEIGNEMENTS					
	Télé-phone	Ouverture	Confort	Nombre de chambres		
				Total	Bains ou douches	
					avec w-c	sans w-c
ANDELOT-EN-MONTAGNE (39110 - Salins-les-Bains)						
* **Hôtel Bourgeois**	**51-43-77**	T-A	♥ 🚗 Ⓟ	16	2	3
39600 - **ARBOIS**						
** **Hôtel des Messageries** ● 2, rue de Courcelles Promenade Pasteur	**66-15-45**	I-III/31-XII	🚗 ⇆	24	10	2
** **Hôtel de Paris** ● 9, rue de l'Hôtel-de-Ville	**66-05-67**	15-III-15-XI	♥ 🚗 Ⓟ ⇆	23	15	3
* **Hôtel de la Poste** 71, Grande-Rue	**66-13-22**	Renseignements non communiqués				

T-A	All the year.
♥	Garden.
♫	Tennis court.
⌓	Swiming pool.
Ⓟ	Parking.
🚗	Garage.
⇆	Dog admitted.
↓↑	Lift.
PI	On seashore.
H	Rooms easy of access to the physically handicapped.
Po	On the port.
M	Sea view.
R	On river bank.
K	Room with kitchnett.
D	On Request.
Incl.	Included.
S. R.	No restaurant.
C	A la carte.

▶ **12** Write a letter of complaint to a French agency called 'Vacances pour Tous' about the gîte you rented in France. What items or conveniences are missing? What was not working? Was anything dirty? You may use the attractions mentioned in the previous question to give you some ideas.

▶ **13** Write a letter to a French friend, describing what you like about your holiday home, e.g. its situation, its appearance, its amenities. You can use the information given in question 12 to give you some ideas.

14 a Using the key given, describe the attractions offered
by one of these campsites.

ALPES-MARITIMES (06) Tél. 16/93

Les normes correspondant aux étoiles figurent en page 9 et la signification des symboles en page 7

ANTIBES (06600) 22 km de Nice
Les Embruns ★★★★ — Rte de Biot, à 3 km de la ville, plage à 100 m. Tél. 33.52.76. Ouvert du
1/4 au 6/9. 0,50 ha. 50 E. Loc. carav., bungalows. Plat, herbeux. ♣♣ □ ⊚ ⊕ 🚿 🛁 ♨ A prox. : 🐟 🐬
🛶 ⚓
Les Frênes ★★★★ — Quartier de la Brague à 600 m de la Plage. Tél. 33.36.52. Ouvert du 1/6 au
30/9. 2 ha. 110 E. Plat, herbeux. ♣♣ □ 🚿 ♨ 🛁 ⚓ A 100 m : 🎾
Les Mimosas ★★★★ — Par N.7, à 4 km N de la ville, bd des Groules, mer à 400 m. Tél.
33.52.76. Ouvert du 1/4 au 15/9. 0,30 ha. 17 E. Loc. carav. En terrasse, sablonneux. ♣♣ □ 🚿 ⊕ Ⓡ
A prox. : 🏊 🐟 🛶 - 82 : forfait 43 et 45/2 pers. - 8,50/pers. suppl.
Fontmerle ★★★ — Chemin de Fontmerle, à 500 m de la N.7 et à 1,2 km de la plage. Tél. 33.02.83.
Ouvert de 1/3 au 1/10. Loc. bungalows. 0,58 ha. 35 E. En terrasse, herbeux. ♣♣ □ 🚿 🐕̸ 🎾 Ⓡ
Le Logis de la Brague ★★★ — R.N. 75 (face gare de Biot). Tél. 33.54.72. Ouvert du 1/5 au
30/9. 1,60 ha. 130 E. Plat, herbeux. ♣ □ ⊚ 🚿 ♨ 🛁 ⚓ ✕ 🍽 A 100 m : 🐟 🛶
Le Pylône ★★★ — A 1,5 km N, rte de Biot. Tél. 33.54.98. Permanent. 10 ha. 800 E. Bord de la
Brague. Plat, herbeux. ♣ ⊚ ♨ 🛁 ✕ 🍽 🐟

	Significance of the symbols
♣	Partly shady
♣♣	Very shady
□	Limited space
⊚	Electric outlets
⊕	Triple outlets for caravans
🚿	Hot showers
🛁	Hot water at every point
♨	Some places of hot water
🛒	Shopping on the premises
🍺	Bar/refrestments on the premises
✕	Restaurant/snack on the premises
🍽	Cooked meals on the premises
🐟	Fishing
🐬	Bathing ground
🏊	Swimming pool
🎾	Tennis
⛵	Sailing/windsurfing/ schoolsailing
🐕̸	Dogs Forbiden
Ⓡ	Reservation
Ⓡ̸	No reservation

b Write a letter to the campsite at Fontmerle, booking a
pitch for a tent and a car for one week in August. Say
there will be two people. Ask how much it costs per
week. If you have space, enquire about campsite
facilities and how far it is to the town centre.

c Write a letter to the campsite at Les Mimosas, booking
a site for a caravan and a car for a fortnight in April.
Say there will be two adults and one child. Ask how
much it will cost, and how far it is to the station. If
you have space, ask about campsite facilities.

15 Write an account of a week-end's walking, camping,
and canoeing holiday you went on from Tréguier to
Paimpol. Base your account on the map and
information given, and include a use you found for each
of the items of personal equipment listed.

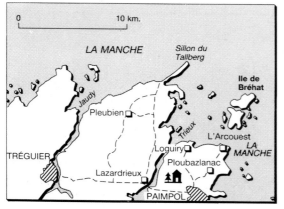

auberge de jeunesse
Château de Kerraoul   22500 PAIMPOL   ☎ 96.20.83.60

Week-end RANDONNEE
- Un week-end randonnée: de Tréguier à Paimpol.
- Pour les initier au Kayak de mer.
- Découverte de l'estuaire du Jaudy et de l'archipel de Bréhat.
- Camping et préparation des repas en commun.
- Du premier jour avant midi au dernier jour dans l'après-midi.

EQUIPEMENT PERSONNEL:

– vieux pulls.	– duvet.
– collant épais.	– lampe de poche.
– tennis ou chaussons néopre.	– maillot de bain.
– K-way.	– pharmacie individuelle.

▶ **16 a** Write a brief description of the geographical situation of each hotel, using the sketch maps given.

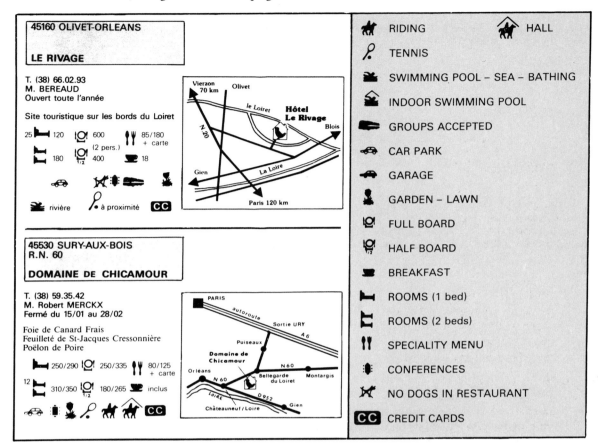

45160 OLIVET-ORLEANS

LE RIVAGE

T. (38) 66.02.93
M. BEREAUD
Ouvert toute l'année

Site touristique sur les bords du Loiret

25 ⊨ 120   🍴 600   🍴 85/180
             (2 pers.)   + carte
⊨ 180   🍴 400   ☕ 18
       1/2

🚗   🐕🚦🚌   ♨

♨ rivière   🎾 à proximité   **CC**

Map: Vierzon 70 km, Olivet, le Loiret, **Hôtel Le Rivage**, N 20, Blois, Gien, La Loire, Paris 120 km

---

45530 SURY-AUX-BOIS
R.N. 60

DOMAINE DE CHICAMOUR

T. (38) 59.35.42
M. Robert MERCKX
Fermé du 15/01 au 28/02

Foie de Canard Frais
Feuilleté de St-Jacques Cressonnière
Poëlon de Poire

⊨ 250/290   🍴 250/335   🍴 80/125
                           + carte
12 ⊨ 310/350   🍴 180/265   ☕ inclus
         1/2

🚗 ⚡ 🌸 🎾 🐎 🐫   **CC**

Map: PARIS, autoroute, Sortie URY, A 6, Puiseaux, **Domaine de Chicamour**, N 60, Montargis, Orléans, N 60, Bellegarde du Loiret, Loire, D 952, Châteauneuf / Loire, Gien

Key:
🐫 RIDING   🏠 HALL
🎾 TENNIS
🏊 SWIMMING POOL – SEA – BATHING
🏊 INDOOR SWIMMING POOL
🚌 GROUPS ACCEPTED
🚗 CAR PARK
🚗 GARAGE
🌸 GARDEN – LAWN
🍴 FULL BOARD
🍴 HALF BOARD
☕ BREAKFAST
⊨ ROOMS (1 bed)
⊨ ROOMS (2 beds)
🍴 SPECIALITY MENU
⚡ CONFERENCES
🐕 NO DOGS IN RESTAURANT
CC CREDIT CARDS

▶▶ **b** Using the key to help you, write a description of the attractions offered by these hotels.

▶▶ **17** The set of pictures depict Anton's first day at work in a hotel. Imagine you are Anton, and write an account of your first day. Was it interesting? tiring? enjoyable?

7 Food and drink

Useful verbs

I'd like . . . j'aimerais . . .; je voudrais . . .
I feel like . . . j'ai envie de . . .
I'll have . . . je prends . . .
I need . . . il me manque
will you . . . voulez-vous . . .

Useful phrases

cover charge le couvert
enjoy your meal! bon appétit!
good health! cheers! à la tienne!, à la vôtre!
in addition en sus, en plus
that's enough ça suffit
tipping not allowed pourboire interdit
what would you like next? et pour suivre?/et ensuite?

Describing food

appetizing appétissant
delicious délicieux
burnt brûlé
just right à point
overcooked trop cuit
thoroughly cooked bien cuit
too salty trop salé
too sweet trop sucré
underdone (*of meat*) saignant

The menu

drink la boisson
main course (*served with vegetables*) le plat garni
salad les crudités (*f*)
today's special le plat du jour

---

1 A courier making out these lists has mixed up the words in French. Can you rewrite them in the correct order?

2 You are stranded on a desert island with only bananas to eat. Write down ten things you'd like to eat when you are rescued.

3 Imagine the three most unappetising foods you can mix together in one sandwich, e.g. marmalade, toothpaste, and sardines. Write down five more ideas for sandwich fillings!

4 Make out two short menus of five words each:
  a for a children's party
  b for an evening meal in a restaurant.

5 You are alone in your pen-friend's house when his/her mother phones. Six guests are coming to dinner and she has been delayed, so she asks your pen-friend to do some things for her. Write down her message in French.

> buy some red and white wine
> buy some bread and cakes
> buy some garlic and tomatoes
> buy some ice-cream and put it into the freezer

MEAT	VIANDE
cold meats	*boeuf*
mutton	*rôti de*
veal	*charcuterie*
lamb	*porc*
beef	*mouton*
pork	*veau*
roast	*agneau*

VEGETABLES	LÉGUMES
garlic	*chou*
rice	*carottes*
mushrooms	*haricots verts*
runner beans	*aïl*
green peas	*chou-fleur*
carrots	*champignons*
cauliflower	*riz*
cabbage	*petits pois*

DESSERTS	DESSERT
ice-cream	*ananas*
stewed fruit	*raisins*
fritters	*glace*
grapes	*compôte*
pineapple	*beignets*

take the meat out of the fridge
set the table
put the meat in the oven
cut the tomatoes into pieces
put the cakes on a plate
peel some potatoes

6 What do you think is in this shopping bag? You have just bought 15 items for a typical English meal which you are going to prepare for your friends in France. What are they?

7 The instructions for these recipes for a 'fluo' party come from the French magazine *Podium*. Replace the pictures with words to complete the recipes.

CROQU'A BILLY

Mélanger 30g. de [🧀] avec 3 carrés demi-sel, 15g. de [🧈] 25g. de [🥜] pilées; étalez sur du [🍞] et passez à un [🔥] très chaud une dizaine de minutes. [🔪] en ▢▢▢ ou en △△△; décorez d'une rondelle de [🍎].

MIX FRAIS ORANGE

Pour 6 verres. Le cocktail doux des fins des soirées. Peler deux 🍊🍊, retirez-en les ⋮⋮ et le coeur. Pressez deux grosses 🍊🍊. Mixez les 🍊🍊 de 🍊 avec le jus d'🍊, 1 litre d' 🚰 et deux 🥄 à soupe de 🧊🧊. Buvez-le "on the rocks" entre deux rocks. En général, ça les fait craquer.

49

8 This family is going to France, and would like you to give them the French words for their favourite foods.

Mike

Jill

David

9 Write the menu for the restaurant 'Au Pommier.'
  a for lunch
  b for dinner.
There should be three sections for each meal:
    soup, salad, pâté
    main dish—meat, fish, vegetables
    cheese, fruit, cakes, ices, etc.
Name about five items for each section.

pour reserver

326-26-45

« AU POMMIER »

22, rue de Vaugirard, Paris (6ᵉ)

pour   seulement

_DEJEUNER

_ DINER   **88**,₀₀ frs.

  aux chandelles   avec VIN et CAFE
avec musique d'ambiance   **TOUT COMPRIS**

entre le SENAT et le Théâtre de l'ODEON -

- face aux Jardins du LUXEMBOURG -

10 a List in French what items of food and drink you might buy at this store for:

1 a picnic
2 a party
3 a family week-end.

Choose ten items for each occasion.

b With a partner, who will be the shop assistant, invent dialogues based on the above items of food and drink. As each item is requested, the assistant should ask a question such as 'How much do you want?' 'What sort of bread/cakes/meat do you want?' or should state the price of what s/he is selling, e.g. 'C'est à dix francs le kilo'.

11 Some friends of yours have won a prize of a week-end in Paris, which includes dinner in a French restaurant. Can you prepare them for the trip by giving them the French for the following useful phrases?

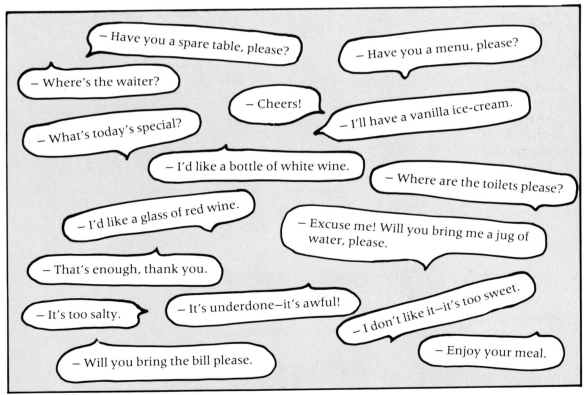

– Have you a spare table, please?

– Have you a menu, please?

– Where's the waiter?

– Cheers!

– I'll have a vanilla ice-cream.

– What's today's special?

– I'd like a bottle of white wine.

– Where are the toilets please?

– I'd like a glass of red wine.

– Excuse me! Will you bring me a jug of water, please.

– That's enough, thank you.

– It's too salty.

– It's underdone–it's awful!

– I don't like it–it's too sweet.

– Will you bring the bill please.

– Enjoy your meal.

12 Send a postcard to your French friend, describing a delicious meal you had the night before at a restaurant in Paris.

13 Write a letter to the chef of a French hotel, asking for work in the kitchen there. Mention a few dishes that you know how to make. If you have space, give any relevant experience and personal information, such as your age, and ability to speak foreign languages. Ask how many hours per day you would have to work, and whether accommodation is available.

14 The Barker family were visiting the Café Ananas, whose menu you can see reproduced here. The waiter was English, so he scribbled their orders down in English. Look at the order below. Decide what the French equivalents are on the menu, and work out the bill.

salad   x 2
ham — Paris
garlic   sausage
pâté

steak + chips   x 2
lamb cutlets
sirloin steak + chips
chateaubriand steak + chips

goats milk cheese
yoghurt
chocolate ice-cream
strawberry tart
Himalaya

Café Brasserie
L'ANANAS
19 AVENUE FRAISERIE

Crudités en Salade	8.05
Pâté de campagne, saucisson sec et à l'ail	9.10
Jambon de Bayonne 'beurre Cornichons'	24.20
Jambon de Paris ,, ,,	17.50

Service continu de 11h.30 à 20h.	PLAT DU JOUR	de 11h.30 à 20h. Fermé samedi et dimanche

Côtes d'agneaux garnies	32.30
Faux filet, pommes frites	32.00
Bifteck, ,, ,,	32.20
Chateaubriant ,, ,,	32.20
Salade	5.32

Fromages:
Gruyère 9.00   Camembert 8.05   Chèvre 9.40
Avec beurre 1.30 de supplément
Yaourt 5.15

Fruits de saison: pomme, orange 5.35
Tartes maison 8.00   Tartes aux fraises 9.00
Crème caramel 6.35   Chantilly 7.50

Nos glaces:
Himalaya 19.90   Glaces assorties 8.05
Mystère 13.00   Parfait 9.65

SERVICE 15% NON COMPRIS

---

15 Write a menu of 15 items for the board outside this cafe. There should be sandwiches, snacks, and drinks, complete with prices.

16 Notice how the restaurant 'La Louisiane' provides a sample 'Brunch Américain', giving the English menu on the left and the French equivalent on the right. Do the same for:

a an English afternoon tea menu

b an English lunch menu.

17 Imagine you are the marketing manager for the 'Brasserie Löwenbräu' featured below. Write some publicity material advertising the restaurant: describe (from the map) how near it is to some famous sights, and describe a typical menu. Remind the customers of the hours of opening, and say what further attractions may be offered in the evenings, e.g. cabaret, disco.

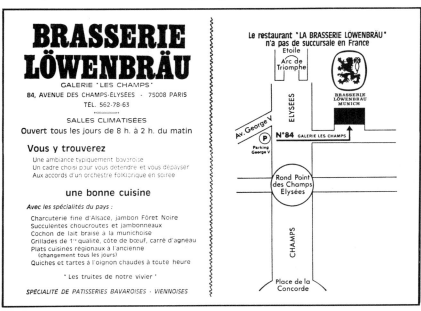

8 Shopping

Shops and stores

dairy   la crémerie
delicatessen, pork butcher's   la charcuterie
greengrocer's   chez le marchand de fruits/de légumes
grocer's   une alimentation, une épicerie
hypermarket   un hypermarché
self-service store   le libre-service
shopping centre   le centre commercial
supermarket   le supermarché

Complaints

	dark		foncé
	dear		cher (chère)
it's	**light** (*in colour*)	c'est	clair
too	**light** (*in weight*)	trop	léger (légère)
	narrow, tight		étroit
	wide		large

to complain   faire une réclamation (contre qn); se plaindre (de qch)

What's it made of?

	cotton		en coton
	leather		en cuir
it's	**nylon**	c'est	en nylon
	plastic		en plastique
	silk		en soie
	wool		en laine

Questions

anything else?   et avec ça?
how much is it?   c'est (à) combien?
is it all right?   ça va?
what colour?   de quelle couleur?
what's the difference?   quelle est la différence?
what's your size   quelle est votre pointure/taille?
have you anything cheaper?   avez-vous quelque chose de moins cher?

---

1 a You were shopping for presents in a French hypermarket when you lost your shopping list. Use the pictures below to help you write it out again.

b You lost your shopping bag, and had to tell the French police what was in it. Make the list from the following pictures.

2 Complete this sentence for each of the pictured items.
On va chez le/à la . . . . . . pour acheter un/une/ des . . . . . .

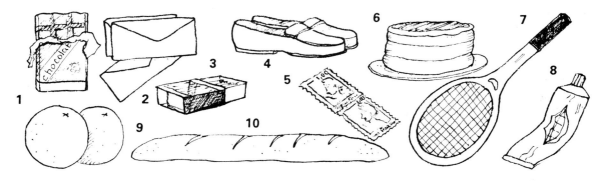

3 Write sentences describing what is wrong with each of the following articles. Use the vocabulary to help you.

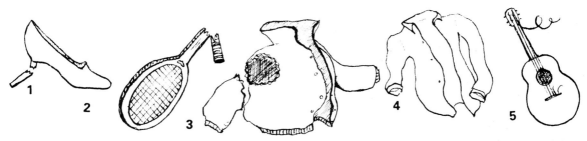

n'a pas de   trop   le talon   court
la manche   la corde   le manche

4 What do you think these people would buy in a
supermarket? Write down six items for each person.

1   2   3   4   5

5 Describe the articles in this shop, and say where they are,
e.g. on which shelf, on the left or right, on the floor, etc.

6 You have just arrived in France, and find that you need a
toothbrush, matches, a newspaper, some bread, and an
umbrella. Write down in French the names of these
articles, and the name of the shop at which you will buy
each one.

7 You are going with three friends to a sports shop in France. Each one of you is interested in a different sport. Make out a list in French of what each of you might buy. This may include suitable clothes. Think of 15 items in all.

8 a You are nearing the end of your holiday in France, and you haven't yet written to your friends. Make out in French a list of five items which you must go and buy for this purpose.

b Your family has sent you out shopping in France. Your father has a headache, your mother would like to shampoo her hair, your brother needs some soap and a deodorant, and you need some toothpaste. Make out a list in French of what you are going to buy, so that you will have no difficulty at the chemist's.

9 You are staying in France with your pen-friend. The father phones home to say that he has been delayed at the office, and therefore cannot do the shopping (illustrated below). He asks you to do it for him. Write down in French what you have to get and where you must go for it.

10 Write a postcard in French to your pen-friend, saying why you are sending this particular postcard, and describing what you have bought at this shop.

▶ ▶ **11** Write a letter to your French friend, in which you thank him/her for a previous letter. Go on to describe a frustrating shopping expedition, when you couldn't obtain any of the articles you wanted. Clothes were either the wrong colour or the wrong size, shoes were the wrong size, other articles weren't in stock, etc.

▶ ▶ **12** Write a letter in French to the mother of your French friend, with whom you have been staying recently. Thank her for her hospitality, and describe the reactions of your family and friends to the presents you brought back for them from France.

▶ ▶ **13** Write a Christmas letter to your French friend, sending Christmas greetings, and describing a recent shopping expedition in which you bought presents for your family and friends. If you have space, say that you are sending him/her a present by separate post.

▶ ▶ **14** Write a letter of complaint to a shop at which you bought an article which has turned out to be of poor quality, e.g. a sweater which shrank or a watch that didn't keep time. Describe what's wrong and ask for a free repair or your money back. If you have space, give details about when and where (e.g. which counter in a large department store) you made your purchase. Describe the assistant who served you, and the claims s/he made for this article.

▶ ▶ **15** Write an account in French of a shopping expedition you made in France to buy souvenirs and presents. Use the shopping list below. (You may add extra details of your own.)

> *Prisunic*
>
> Dad – wallet.   Grandparents – wine.
> Jane – doll.   Chris – key ring.
>
> *Also need*
>
> Writing paper, envelopes, postcards, magazines, camera film.

9 Services

The post office

how much is it to send . . .?   c'est combien pour envoyer . . .?

I'd like . . . please   je voudrais . . . s'il vous plaît

give me . . . please   donnez-moi . . . s'il vous plaît

three 2-franc stamps   trois timbres à deux francs

one 50-centime stamp   un timbre à cinquante centimes

which counter?   (à) quel guichet?

---

1 a A new post office clerk was told to slot the French and English words into this sign to help the English customers, but he got rather mixed up. Can you help him out?

b When you have sorted out these lists, make up a question and answer using each word. For oral work, choose a partner; one of you can be the clerk and the other the customer. Remember to swap roles.

P.T.T.	
Post Office	Boîte aux lettres
Parcel	Imprimé
Letterbox	Mandat
Weight	Paquet
Money order	Adresse
Printed matter	Bureau de poste
Address	Poids
Poste Restante	Par avion
Identity card	Journal
By air mail	Récépissé
Postage stamps	Poste restante
Newspaper	Pièce d'identité
Registered	Réclamation
Receipt	Recommandé
Claim	Timbres

2 a You are about to go to the post office in France. First make notes on what you want to say.
   a You wish to post a parcel to England by air.
   b It's fragile, and it's urgent.
   c Do they have a price list for parcels?
   d You also want five stamps at two francs each.

b With a partner, make up a conversation using the sentences from question 2a. One of you is the clerk and one the customer.

3 You wish to send £5 as a birthday present to your English friend while you are living in France. Copy out and fill in the form below.

COUPON	ADMINISTRATION DES POSTES	MANDAT DE POSTE INTERNATIONAL

COUPON
(Peut être détaché par le bénéficiaire)

ADMINISTRATION DES POSTES DE FRANCE

MANDAT DE POSTE INTERNATIONAL

Cours du change [1]

Montant en monnaie étrangère (en chiffres)

Montant en monnaie étrangère (en chiffres)

Somme payée [1]

S'il y a lieu application des timbres-poste ou indication de la taxe perçue

Date d'émission

(En toutes lettres)

Nom et adresse de l'expéditeur

Nom du bénéficiaire

Rue et n°

Lieu de destination

Pays de destination

[1] A porter par l'Administration de paiement lorsqu'elle opère la conversion.

Timbre du bureau d'émission

Timbre du bureau d'émission

Indications du bureau d'émission

N° du mandat

Somme versée

FF

Bureau

Date

N° 1405. - IN 3 112209 M 89 D

Signature de l'agent

DESTINATAIRE

EXPÉDITEUR

MONTANT

FF

Destination

Telephoning

the directory   l'annuaire (*m*)
to lift the receiver   décrocher le combiné
the slot   la fente

to dial the number   composer le numéro
the dialling tone   la tonalité
to hang up   raccrocher

▶ 4 Your French friend has just arrived in England and wishes to make a phone call from an English call box. As s/he cannot speak or read much English, write down in French the stages involved so that s/he can go to the call box alone.

The bank or exchange bureau*

rate of exchange le taux d'échange
to cash a cheque toucher/encaisser un chèque

100-franc note un billet de cent francs
the rest le reste

5 a Your friend Sarah is going to visit a French bank or
exchange bureau. As she doesn't know much French,
write down some useful phrases to help her. Note
down too what the bank clerk may say to her so that
she will understand what she is being asked to do.

She may want to say:
  What is the rate of exchange today?
  I'd like to cash a cheque, please.
  I'd like to change some traveller's cheques.
  Here's my passport.
  I'd like two 100-franc notes and the rest in
    10-franc notes.

The clerk may ask her:
  Can I help you?
  May I see your passport?
  Have you any identification?
  How much do you want?
  How do you want it?
  Will you sign here, please?

b With a partner, make up the sort of conversation that
Sarah and the bank clerk might hold. Try to make up
variations on the theme, e.g. Sarah may not have her
passport with her, or she may wish to cash a different
amount of money.

6 Sarah is about to visit the bank again. Can you write
down the French for the following sentences to help her
out?
  a I'd like to buy some traveller's cheques. Which counter
  is it, please?
  b What is the exchange rate at today's price?
  c I'd like to buy traveller's cheques to the value of £30
  sterling.
  d I think you have made a mistake.
  e Where must I sign?
  f Please may I have a receipt?

7 You are doing a project on French banking. Write a letter
to a French bank such as the 'Crédit Lyonnais',
explaining this, and asking for information to help you.
Ask for samples of forms for making credit transfers and
for buying (**achat de**) traveller's cheques and foreign
currency. Ask if they issue (**donner** or **fournir**) credit
cards. Ask how many branches (**succursales**) of 'Crédit
Lyonnais' there are in France, and if they have branches
in other countries too. If you have space, ask one or two
questions of your own.

*Not all syllabuses include the bank, lost property, and repairs in their
requirements at basic level for the written part of the French examination,
although most of them do so for comprehension and oral work.

At the garage

battery la batterie
brake le frein
radiator le radiateur
spare wheel la roue de secours
tyre le pneu

to check vérifier

to clean nettoyer
to fix fixer, arranger

how much is it to . . .? c'est combien pour . . .?
isn't working ne marche pas/est en panne

▶ **8 a** Write down the sort of questions you would need to ask if you took this car to a French garage. Besides the problems you can see, there is no spare wheel, and the brakes don't work.

▶▶ **b** With a partner, play the parts of a car-owner and a garage mechanic. See how many questions and answers you can make up, based on this picture.

9 You are staying in France at the house of your French friend, and you have just received a phone call from your friend's mother. She says she will arrive home late, at about 8 p.m. The reason for this is that she has a burst tyre, and is waiting for it to be repaired at a garage in the outskirts of Paris. You are just about to go out, write down the gist of this message for the family when they return.

10 You are alone in your French friend's house when the phone rings. Write up your notes in French to give to your friend's father.

> M. Boulogne —
> Garage mechanic rang from Citroën garage in town.
> - Car still broken down.
> - Waiting for new radiator.
> - Can M. Boulogne collect car on Friday?

11 Your French friend has phoned you at his house in France to tell you why he hasn't come home yet. (The pictures below explain the situation.) Write down the gist of the message in French, for his parents, and add that he doesn't know what time he will arrive home.

Having things repaired or cleaned

electrician   un électricien
dry cleaner's   le nettoyage à sec, le dégraisseur
garage mechanic   le garagiste
plumber   le plombier

shoe repairer   le cordonnier
dirty   sale
torn   déchiré
to repair   réparer

12 a Using the pictures below, say what is wrong with each object, and where you should ask for help.

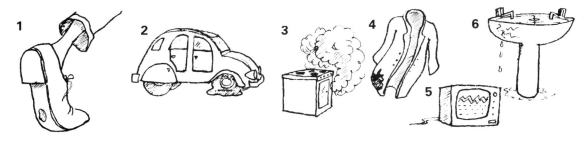

b Using the same pictures, write a story entitled 'Une journée désastreuse'.

▶ ▶ **13** Expand the following telegram into a full account of the incident, describing the place where Brigitte is stranded, and what she has done and is going to do while waiting for repairs to be made. If you like, you can imagine you are Brigitte and write the story in the first person.

```
IMPOSSIBLE D'ARRIVER AUJOURD'HUI - EN PANNE - BRIGITTE
```

14 You are alone in your French friend's house when the phone rings. Write up the message in French to give to Madame Lebrun.

Madame Lebrun

Message from dry cleaner's. Coat you left there yesterday is torn, but could be repaired.
Please phone them tomorrow.

Lost property

dark blue	bleu foncé	**square**	carré
light blue	bleu clair	**wide**	large
empty	vide		
full	plein	**made of gold**	en or
long	long (longue)	**made of leather**	en cuir
narrow	étroit	**made of metal**	en métal
new	neuf (neuve)	**made of nylon**	en nylon
rectangular	rectangulaire	**made of plastic**	en plastique
round	rond	**made of silver**	en argent
short	court	**made of wood**	en bois

15 You are about to phone the lost property office at the Gare du Nord, as you have left a suitcase in the waiting room there. Write notes in French on what you are going to say. Include the following points:
   a State your name and address.
   b Say what you lost, its colour, size, and material.
   c Say briefly what it contained.
   d Say where you have left it.

▶ **16** Write a letter to the lost property office at the Gare Maritime, Calais, saying that you lost a handbag or wallet there. Describe its size, colour, material, age, value, and contents. If you have space, say when and where it was lost, describe the circumstances in which it was lost, ask if it has been handed in, and enquire what you must do next.

17 You are working in a French lost property office, and
you have to make notes on the articles people have lost.
Describe the lost articles pictured below, following the
example shown on the form.

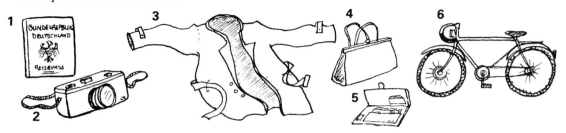

Date de la perte :	**Lieu de la perte (1)**
Heure de la perte :	~~Dans le métro, ligne Nᵒ~~
OBJET PERDU	~~Dans l'autobus, ligne Nᵒ~~
Qu'avez-vous perdu ? *une montre*	~~Dans un taxi~~
	— Dans un établissement public (2)
Décrivez l'objet :	~~Sur la voie publique (2)~~
1 - Forme, couleur : *carré*	
....	*dans le cinéma*
....	
....	**Inscrivez vos Nom, prénom et adresse**
2 - Contenu : —	M. Mᵐᵉ Mˡˡᵉ (1) ....
....	
....	Demeurant : ....
....	
3 - Autres détails caractéristiques :	Téléphone : ....
en or	Profession : ....
nom dessus : Annie Redor	
....	Paris, le : ....
4 - Valeur de l'objet : *F 1.500*	Signature : ....
Imp. S T 9509 C 3-70 **Voir au dos**	(1) Rayer les mentions inutiles.
	(2) Précisez l'endroit.

▶▶ **18** Write a reply to a letter from a person who has lost
something in the Parisian café where you are working.
Say whether or not you have found it, and what they
should do about it.

▶▶ **19** Continue the following letter.

Paris, le 15 mars

Cher Francis,
Merci beaucoup de ta lettre. Je t'écris pour te raconter
une aventure curieuse qui m'est arrivée l'autre jour à la
Poste . . .

10 Health and safety

Feeling ill

I have	**backache**	au dos
	a headache	à la tête
	toothache j'ai mal	aux dents
	stomach	à l'estomac /
	ache	au ventre

my arm hurts j'ai mal au bras
my eyes hurt j'ai mal aux yeux
my leg hurts j'ai mal à la jambe
I feel sick j'ai mal au coeur
I have a sore throat j'ai mal à la gorge

I am air/car/seasick j'ai le mal de l'air/de la route/de mer
I have a cold/flu j'ai un rhume/la grippe
I have a temperature j'ai de la température/de la fièvre
I have sunstroke j'ai un coup de soleil/une insolation

On the street

to be careful faire attention
to brake freiner
to cross traverser
to collide with entrer en collision avec
to have priority avoir la priorité sur
to hurt blesser
to knock down renverser, écraser
to overtake dépasser
to stop s'arrêter

driving licence le permis de conduire
highway code le code de la route
identification la pièce d'identité
(red) traffic lights les feux (rouges) (*m*)
be careful! attention!
you're going to . . . vous allez . . .
I didn't know that . . . je ne savais pas que . . .
I'm sorry je m'excuse/je suis désolé
you must (not) il (ne) faut (pas)

1 Copy out this chart and write in what you would prescribe for these conditions.
Below the chart there is some vocabulary to help you.

Mal aux dents	– prendre de l'aspirine et aller chez le dentiste
Mal à la tête	– . . . .
Mal au ventre	– . . . .
Mal aux yeux	– . . . .
Mal au dos	– . . . .
Jambe cassée	– . . . .
Mal au coeur	– . . . .
Doigt gonflé	– . . . .
De la fièvre	– . . . .
Une insolation	– . . . .

cream la crème
injection une piqûre
medicine le médicament
mixture le sirop
pills des pilules/des cachets
prescription une ordonnance

to go to bed straight away aller au lit tout de suite
to go to the dentist's/the optician's aller chez le dentiste/l'opticien
to stay in bed for . . . days garder le lit pendant . . . jours

2 Make a list of 15 items you'll need from the chemist prior to going down to the Mediterranean coast with your friend.

3 a Make a list of all the traffic violations and pedestrian mistakes you can spot in the picture below. Full sentences are not necessary.

b With a partner, have a short conversation about each of the above situations. One of you (the policeman) should draw attention to what is wrong ('Attention, Monsieur/Madame! Il ne faut pas conduire si vite!') and the other one should try to think of a convincing excuse ('Pardon, Monsieur l'agent, je . . .')

c Using the vocabulary on p.66, write ten 'rules of the road' in French.

4 Your pen-friend is taken ill while you are staying in France, and his/her parents are at work. You jot down the symptoms and then phone one of the parents. Make a note of what they tell you to do. Write 15 words.

5 Your French pen-friend is staying with you but is out shopping. You have toothache and are going to the dentist's. Leave a note in French to explain to your friend where everyone is. The details are as follows:

Your father won't be home for dinner because he's had a car accident. He's not hurt, but is at the police station . . .

Your mother will be home about 6 p.m. She has gone to the hospital because she's hurt her arm. It's nothing serious.

You don't have an appointment at the dentist's and so think you'll have to wait a long time. You'll catch a bus home.

6 Write down what you would say if you wanted to phone the emergency services in France in the following situations.

a There is a fire in the house. Give your address. Say which rooms are affected and that you are alone.

b There has been an accident in the house. State your name, address, and the nature of the accident.

7 You have received the following postcard from your French friend. Write a postcard in reply, wishing him a speedy recovery. If you have space, add a little news.

> Megève, le 6 janvier
>
> Ça te surprend, n'est-ce pas, de recevoir cette carte postale ? C'est que je me suis cassé la jambe sur la piste. Je suis donc au lit, et complètement mélanco. Tu as passé un bon Noël ? Écris-moi bientôt.
>
> Ton ami, Olivier

8 Write a postcard to your French friend describing being seasick on your way home from France.

▶ **9** Write a letter to your French friend saying that you can't go to France as arranged because you are in hospital. If you have space, describe how you came to be there, and how you like it (or not!)

▶▶ **10** Write a letter to your French friend describing a visit to your doctor in England. Your friend will be particularly interested as you had felt unwell during your recent stay in France.

11 Free time and friends

I like/I don't like   j'aime/je n'aime pas
I hate   j'ai horreur de
I detest   je déteste

aerobics   faire de l'aérobic
computer programming   faire de la programmation
cycling   faire du cyclisme
DIY   faire du bricolage
going to parties   aller à des boums
gymnastics/exercises   faire de la gymnastique
playing computer games   jouer à des jeux d'ordinateur
skiing   faire du ski
swimming   faire de la natation
walking   faire des promenades
winter sports   aller aux sports d'hiver

it's amusing, funny   c'est amusant, drôle
it's awful   c'est affreux
it's boring   c'est ennuyeux
it's exciting   c'est passionnant
it' great! fantastic!   c'est chouette! formidable! génial! sensass! super!
it's interesting   c'est intéressant

Types of film

comedies   les films comiques
cops and robbers   les films policiers

films dubbed in French   les films en version française
films with the original sound track   les films en version originale
horror films   les films d'épouvante
romantic films   les films d'amour
cartoons   les dessins animés
documentaries   les documentaires
news   les informations
TV news   le télé-journal

Suggesting a meeting

We can go to the match.   Nous pouvons aller au match.
Suppose we went to the party?   Si on allait à la boum?
Suppose we met at the cinema?   Si on se rencontrait au cinéma?
I suggest a walk/drive.   Je te propose une promenade/une randonnée.

Refusing an invitation

that depends . . .   ça dépend . . .
I'm sorry . . .   je m'excuse/je regrette/je suis désolé
I'm afraid it's impossible   malheureusement, c'est impossible
I can't   je ne peux pas
I'd rather . . .   je préfère . . .

1   How do you think the following people spend their free time? Write in French what each is doing, and say what equipment, clothes, and expenses each will have.

Alain   Brigitte   Sophie   Laurent

Roland   Frédéric   Omar   Sylvie   Nadine   Véronique

2 Write two or three different sentences for each of the following activities, varying the place or the time of each activity, e.g.

> 'Nous pouvons regarder la télévision à la maison.'
> 'Si on regardait la télévision au club?'

You could start off your suggestions by using:
Veux-tu . . .? Tu veux . . .? Tu préfères . . .?

Where?

sports stadium	at home	in town
youth club	sports centre	in the country

3 Someone you don't like very much has asked you out. Take ten different suggestions from question 2, and for each one write a polite refusal in a few words. For example, you may have another engagement, or be ill.

4 This time you would like to go out with the person who has invited you, but either the activity, the time, or the place is not to your liking. Write replies to ten of the suggestions from question 1 again, and for each one come up with an alternative idea, e.g.

> 'Nous pouvons regarder la télévision à la maison.'
> 'Je ne veux pas regarder la télévision. Je préfère aller à la boum.'

5 Write 30 words in French about each of these people, saying how you think each would spend his/her free time and what they would spend their pocket money on.

Jérôme

Christiane

Olivier

Marie-Pierre

6 a You are spending a term at a French school, and have been asked to do a survey of the way some of your class-mates spend their pocket money and their leisure time. You make a chart from your information (see below). Now write it up in the form of a report, using complete sentences in French.

		Corinne	Jean-Marc	Florence	Régis	Carole
GETS	earnings	50F	80F	40F	—	30F
	pocket money	20F	—	60F	30F	40F
SAVES	saves	9F		20F		5F
SPENDS	records	✓	✓	✓	✓	✓
	magazines		✓		✓	
	dancing	✓		✓		✓
	transport		(scooter) ✓			✓
	clothes	✓		✓		✓
	extras	Swimming	football matches	Skating	youth club	parties

b Find a partner, and take it in turns to be interviewer and interviewee. One asks questions in French about the amount of spending money and how it is spent. The other replies as though s/he is one of the young people named above. You could ask also how your interviewee earns money, and if s/he has any hobbies which don't cost much, such as listening to the radio, reading, etc.

7 a You want to ring a new French friend to arrange a meeting. As you are not sure what s/he likes doing, make a list of ten suggestions before making the phone call, e.g.
A huit heures près du cinéma? Si on allait voir un film d'épouvante?

b With a partner, act out the conversation you might have in French on the phone.

8 Make a list in French of how you enjoy — and don't enjoy — spending your leisure time, both in winter and summer. Write a total of 20 suggestions.

En hiver
J'aime . . .
Je n'aime pas . . .
J'ai horreur de . . .

En été
J'aime . . .
Je n'aime pas . . .
J'ai horreur de . . .

9 a Your French pen-friend is coming to spend a fortnight at your house. Make a list in French for his/her benefit of what you can do and see during that time. Make about ten suggestions.

▶ **b** Write a letter to the same French friend, welcoming him/her and putting your list of suggestions into the letter.

10 You are staying in a hostel in France and have had to answer the phone. Leave messages (in French of course!) for the people who were out.

a Christine rang with a message for Paul. She can't meet him outside the cinema tonight, as the car has broken down. She would like him to phone back.

b Dominique rang with a message for Laurent. He can't go to the football match on Saturday, as he has 'flu. Can Laurent go to his house?

c Omar rang with a message for Véronique. He has bought two tickets for the theatre next Tuesday; would she like to go with him? Please phone.

d Sandrine rang with a message for Medgée. Would Medgée like to go shopping with her tomorrow? If so, come to the 'Bonne Amie' at 10 a.m.

11 Write a postcard to your French pen-friend, with whom you have been staying recently, saying that you have left a suitcase in the left-luggage office at the station in his home town. Ask him/her to bring it to England when s/he comes to visit you next month. Apologize for the trouble.

12 Write a postcard to your pen-friend thanking him/her for sending you some photos of your stay that s/he has just had developed. Tell him/her which photos you prefer, and if you have space say that you look forward to going back next year.

13 Write a postcard to your French friend, saying that you are arriving at the bus station in Rouen on 23 October at 6 p.m. Ask if s/he can meet you there.

14 Write a postcard to your French friend, thanking him/her for an invitation to a party, and saying that you will be there at a stated date and time. If you have space, add some news or greeting.

▶ ▶ **15** Write in French a letter of apology for not turning up at an arranged time and place to go to the cinema with a new acquaintance. Say why you couldn't come, and invite the other person to another date instead.

16 a Write a letter introducing yourself to one of the correspondents below, saying why you would like to write to the person. Describe yourself and your interests. If you have space, suggest a suitable meeting.

Laurent Pernot	**Patricia Trommenschlager**	**Christine Leblanc**
Une fille dans chaque port, c'est bon pour les marins, mais moi petit pianiste de jazz de 16 ans qui passe 200 jours par an à voyager pour la musique, j'attends encore les amies de 14 à 18 ans. Photo demandée.	Réclamons 5 garçons de 16 à 18 ans. Ce n'est pas ce que vous croyez: on fonde un orchestre à deux copines, il nous faut des danseurs, une batterie, guitare électrique et orgue. Dans la région.	J'aime vivre dangereusement. Moto, parachutisme, aventures, tout me passionne. La preuve, ne riez pas, je veux être une femme flic plus tard. En attendant je me suis cassé une jambe au ski, n'est pas Sherlock Holmes qui veut. Apprenez-moi.
Carina Falk	**Jean-Pierre Laloye**	**Soldat Bertin J.P.**
Tout le monde parle de la Suède sans la connaître. Moi je peux vous raconter les villes, les forêts, la vie. En Français. Je suis fana de ski et de pop. J'ai 16 ans.	Un: je cherche une fille gourmande, car je suis apprenti pâtissier. Deux: il faut qu'elle aime la moto, j'ai une 125 Honda mono cylindre. Trois: il faut qu'elle ne soit pas moche. Je suis un mignon mitron.	Le drapeau ne flotte pas bien haut pour un piou-piou de 19 ans. Pitié. J'aime pas le kaki.

b One of the above correspondents has written to you suggesting a meeting at a certain time and place, but you don't really want to go. Decline the invitation politely, making a good excuse.

17 a Write a postcard in French to your pen-friend, who is staying in a nearby French town, saying that you have bought two tickets for a pop concert. If s/he would like to go s/he should phone you soon.

b With a partner, act out the phone call in question 17a.

18 Write a thank-you letter to the French family with whom you have just spent a week, thanking them for their hospitality, and mentioning some of the activities you enjoyed while in France.

19 Write in French to a tourist information office in a French town of your choice, asking for maps, town plans, brochures, and programmes of events. If you have space, ask if there are any castles, sites of interest, or museums in the area.

20 Write in French to a tourist information office in a French town of your choice, asking for hotel and campsite lists. Ask if they have any leaflets about excursions or evening entertainment. If you have space, ask about the availability of tennis and other sports.

▶▶ **21 a** Write in French an account of a few days you spent, or plan to spend, in Paris. Base your activities mainly on the advertisements above. Say where you went, what happened, and how you enjoyed it. Or describe what you hope to do, and why.

b Make up a conversation in French with a partner, discussing, on the basis of the above advertisements, what you plan to do during a short holiday in Paris. It will be more lively if you disagree with one another. Try to support your suggestions or disagreements with suitable comments such as 'Ce serait formidable/sensass!', or 'Ah non, ce serait moche/ennuyant!'

▶ **c** Write in French to one of the establishments above, booking tickets, a course of lessons, or a table at a restaurant for a certain date and a stated number of people. If the price is given, say you enclose a cheque for the amount, if this is necessary in advance. If not, ask how much it will cost. If you have space, state any special requests you may have, e.g. at the restaurant you may like to order a birthday cake, or if you are booking tickets, you may want seats near the aisle.

▶ **22** Write a letter to your pen-friend saying that you are sending him/her a birthday present. Say what it is. Send wishes for a happy birthday and add some news if you have space.

23 a Write out the following letter, filling in the gaps according to the illustrations:

Chers Boys et Girls,

Je recherche de toute urgence une 😊 que j'ai rencontrée il y a quinze jours à une soirée dansante. Elle était accompagnée de sa 👦 (je crois) et d'une autre dame plus âgée (peut-être sa 👵). Moi, j'étais avec un 🙂 et j'étais habillé d'un 🧥 en cuir ⬛ et d'un gros 🖐 col roulé gris clair. Je suis brun aux 👀 marrons, les 〰 assez courts.

Elle, portait un 👖 de velours rose clair et un 👕 de la même couleur. J'aimerais beaucoup la revoir pour mieux la connaître. Si elle lit mon message, elle peut m'écrire à *Girls* qui a mon adresse. Merci beaucoup.

Frank

b Write a reply to Frank as though you were the girl he was searching for. Introduce yourself, and say you would like to be his pen-friend.

24 Imagine you are working on the problem page of *OK!* Write a reply (giving plenty of helpful advice!) to one of the following letters:

N.V., Villefranche-sur-Saône: «GROS, LAID ET DESESPERE»

Vous êtes les seuls qui puissiez me comprendre et me conseiller. Aussi, j'espère que vous ne jetterez pas ma lettre. J'ai dix-sept ans. Je suis gros, laid . . . et désespéré. Et si seul. Personne ne veut se montrer en ma compagnie. A mon âge, je n'ai même jamais flirté. Pas normal, n'est-ce pas? Répondez-moi vite.

Eric, Gilles et Stéphane: «NOUS AIMONS TOUS LES TROIS LA MEME FILLE»

Nous espérons que vous ne trouverez pas notre problème ridicule et que vous le publierez dans un prochain numéro de OK! Voilà: nous sommes trois bons copains âgés de seize/dix-sept ans qui . . . aimons la même fille. Elle se prénomme Béatrice et a quinze ans et demi. Elle est superbe, drôle et très sympa. C'est lors d'une boum, il y a un mois, que nous l'avons rencontrée et elle nous a fait litéralement craquer.

Stéphane, Suisse: «MA MERE ME CONSIDERE COMME UN GAMIN»

J'ai seize ans. Mon problème: ma mère me traite en gamin. Elle veut toujours que je sois rentré au plus tard à 21 heures. Cela m'énerve d'autant plus que des «petits» de 8–10 ans, habitant mon quartier, ont l'autorisation de sortir jusqu'à 22 heures et même parfois plus tard. J'ai parlé de cela à ma mère, mais elle est intraitable: c'est 21 heures ou pas de sortie du tout. Quelle vie! Je vous en prie, dites-moi ce que je dois faire pour la raisonner dans un prochain OK!

12 School and work

At school

biology   la biologie
business studies   les cours commerciaux (*m*)
chemistry   la chimie
computer science   l'informatique (*f*)
cricket   le cricket
football   le football
geography   la géographie
history   l'histoire (*f*)
hockey   le hockey
maths   les maths (*f*)
music   la musique
physics   la physique
practical subjects   les travaux manuels (*m*)
rugby   le rugby
swimming   la natation
tennis   le tennis

After school

air hostess   une hôtesse de l'air
clerk, employee   un(e) employé(e)
dentist   le dentiste
driver   le chauffeur
factory   une usine
fireman   le pompier
garage mechanic   le garagiste
job, trade, profession   le métier
nurse   un infirmier/une infirmière
profession   la profession

How long have you been learning French/Spanish/ German?   Depuis combien de temps apprenez-vous le français/l'espagnol/l'allemand?
I've been learning it for five years.   Je l'apprends depuis cinq ans.

redundant: to be made redundant   être mis au chômage
salesman/woman   le vendeur/la vendeuse
secretary   le/la secrétaire
unemployed   en chômage, sans travail

certificate, diploma   le brevet, le certificat, le diplôme
exam   un examen
job   un emploi
marks   les notes (*f*)
school   le lycée, le collège, l'école (*f*)
subject   la matière
timetable   un emploi du temps

to fail an exam   rater
to learn   apprendre
to pass an exam   réussir à un examen
to take an exam   passer un examen

Languages

Dutch   le hollandais
English   l'anglais
French   le français
German   l'allemand
Italian   l'italien
Russian   le russe
Spanish   l'espagnol
Urdu   l'ourdou

---

1 Write about 30 words for each of the following, giving advice to someone who wanted to be:
   a a tennis-player   **c** a doctor
   b a teacher   **d** a pop star
   You may find the following phrases useful:

Il faut | vous intéresser à . . .
passer beaucoup de temps à . . .
étudier les matières suivantes . . .

2 Find the correct answer for each question, then write out question and answer.

—Vous apprenez quelle langue?

—Qu'est-ce que vous écoutez?

—C'est le mot juste?

—Vous l'apprenez depuis combien de temps?

—Voulez-vous parler plus lentement?

—Depuis quatre ans.

—Oui, excusez-moi, je vais recommencer.

—Le français.

—La bande.

—Oui, c'est exact.

3 a For each person, say what their job is and where they work, e.g.

Jean-Luc est professeur. Il travaille dans une école.

1 Jean-Luc **2** Valérie **3** Géraldine **4** François **5** Paul **6** Eric **7** Nathalie **8** Fabienne **9** Robert **10** Stéphanie

b Write down two things the above people do in their jobs. The following vocabulary may help you:

aider	faire des calculs	servir
arracher	faire la vaisselle	soigner
corriger	laver	téléphoner
couper	plomber	vendre
écrire	préparer	

Example: Jean-Luc écrit sur le tableau noir et il corrige les devoirs.

4 What do you think the people in question 3 were like at school? Describe each one, using the following pattern to help you:

Il/elle a _____ ans.

Il/elle aime | les sciences.
| les maths.
| les langues.
| la gymnastique.

Il/elle n'aime pas _____.

Dans _____ ans il/ | le brevet des collèges.
elle va passer | le BT (brevet de
| technicien).
| le BTn (baccalauréat
| de technicien).
| le bac.

5 You are shortly going to interview a French boy or girl. Write down ten questions you plan to ask him/her. You wish to know his/her age, favourite subjects and hobbies, what school and class s/he is in, and what ambitions s/he has for his/her life and career.

OR

You have just interviewed a French boy or girl of your own age about his/her everyday life and career plans. Summarize the results of the interview by filling in details under the following headings:

nom   école
âge   classe
sujets préférés (2)   carrière préférée
passe-temps favoris (2)

6 Write a similar postcard to the one shown here. You too are at a language school, but you are not so hard-working. You are in Spain and spend half an hour a day at the library, and two hours on the beach. You listen to the radio and read magazines. You write nothing and your teacher says you are not making much progress . . . but you are having a wonderful time!

> Lausanne, le 8 août
> Chère Corinne,
>   Me voici en Suisse. Chaque jour je passe deux heures à étudier au collège, et deux heures à parler français. J'écris aussi des compositions.
>   J'écoute les informations à la radio et je lis des journaux sérieux.
>   Mon Prof. dit que je fais beaucoup de progrès.
>   Amicalement,
>   Karen.

▶ **7** Write a letter of application for one of these jobs, stating your qualifications and experience. If you have space, say why this job particularly interests you.

Avoué à la Cour ch. pour 15 sept.-15 janv., dactylo expérimentée. Ecr. S.N.P. n° 1024, B.P. 907, 76023 Rouen Cedex.

Ch. caissière temps partiel pour magasin produits surgelés, Bihorel. Envoyer C.V. et photo, M. ROUSSET, 172, rue Eau-de-Robec, 76000, Rouen.

Recherche pour Paris 16°:
EMPLOYEE MAISON
Nourrie, logée. Aura à s'occuper d'un nouveau-né. Tél. Bellot: 45.24.22.02.

Ch. apprentie vendeuse boulangerie-pâtisserie. Tél. 35.17.13.99.

Société location de voitures et camionnettes recrute secrétaire hôtesse. Ecrire avec réf. à S.N.P. n° 15067, B.P. 907, 76023 Rouen Cedex.

---

biS TRAVAIL TEMPORAIRE
SECRETAIRE
Bilingue anglais
Se prés. avec certif. trav., 5, rue du 11-Novembre, 27400 Louviers. Tél. 32.40.07.99.

Pharmacie, 25 km Rouen, ch. apprenti(e), niv. 1re. Tél. 35.33.23.22.

Ch. pompiste temps partiel. Ecrire M. Rollo, 12, rue Bosquet, 76001, Rouen.

Société de service Rouen recherche H. ou F. titulaire Bac informatique (H.). Travail poste 2×8. Envoyer C.V. + lettre manuscrite et photo à S.N.P. n° 15070, B.P. 907, 76023 Rouen Cedex.

B.P. boîte postale
certif. certificat
C.V. curriculum vitae
F. femme
H. homme
niv. niveau
réf. référence(s)
se prés. se présente
tél. téléphonez
trav. travail

▶ **8** Imagine that you have put in the paper one of the advertisements below. Expand your short advertisement into a letter of application, giving details of your education and experience. If you have space, say why you are particularly interested in the job.

J.F., B.T.S. action commerciale, B.T. représentation, expér. secrétariat, ch. poste stable. Tél. 32.44.47.24.

J.F., rech. place employée de bureau dactylo. Tél. 35.62.58.59.

Très urgent. J.H., sér., dynamique, possédant permis de conduire, rech. emploi indif. Tél. M. Roger LAINE, 35.70.13.34.

Jeune homme, vendeur dans grande surface rayons épicerie, liquides, produits frais, cherche emploi:

VENDEUR
Tél. 44.22.47.77

Aide soignante, sérieuse réf. contrôle, ch. place de garde-malade chez pers. âgées à mi-temps ou à la journée. Tél. 35.71.35.21.

---

ch. cherche
expér. expérimenté(e)
J.F. jeune femme
J.H. jeune homme
pers. personnes
rech. recherche
réf. référence(s)
sér. sérieux

9 Write a letter to a language school in France, applying for a place there. Give details of the date you want to arrive, and how long you wish to stay. Ask how much it will cost.

If you have space, say how long you have been learning French, and why you want to learn more French. Say what previous experience you have had of France or French studies.

10 Imagine you are writing your first letter to a new French pen-friend. Introduce yourself, and describe in particular your interests at school, what you want to do as a career, and how you plan to achieve this. If you have space, ask your new friend about his/her interests and career plans.

11 Here is a letter from the French magazine *Boys et Girls*. Imagine you are Geneviève and write a suitable reply.

Patricia 15 ans
«Quel métier choisir?»

Chère Geneviève,
Je suis en classe de troisième. Je me débrouille assez bien puisque je vais passer en seconde. Seulement je m'interroge sur mon avenir. Je ne sais pas quel métier choisir. Peux tu m'aider?

12 Write an account of your first day at a new job. Where was it? What time did you arrive? What was your place of work like? Describe the other employees and your boss. How did they behave? Did you make any mistakes?

English–French vocabulary

If, when looking up a word, you find that two meanings are given, and you are not sure which one to use, check in a French–English dictionary.

able: to be able pouvoir
about environ; **to be about to** être sur le point de
above au-dessus (de), en haut
abroad à l'étranger
absent absent
absolutely absolument
accent un accent
to **accept** accepter
accident un accident
account le compte
accurate exact, correct
to **accuse** accuser
acquaintance: to make someone's acquaintance faire la connaissance de qn
active actif (-ive)
activity une activité
actor un acteur
actress une actrice
addition: in addition en sus, en plus
address une adresse
to **admit** laisser entrer; **to be admitted** être admis
to **adore** adorer
adult un(e) adulte
advance: in advance en avance
advertisement une annonce; **small ad** une petite annonce
to **advise** conseiller
afraid: to be afraid avoir peur; **I'm afraid so!** hélas oui! **I'm afraid not!** hélas non!
after après, au bout de
afternoon un après-midi
afterwards ensuite
again encore, de nouveau
against contre
age un âge; **how old is**

he? quel âge a-t-il?
to **agree, get on together** s'entendre
agricultural agricole
agriculture l'agriculture (f)
air: by air par avion; **open-air** en plein air
alas hélas
alive vivant
all, every tout
all year toute l'année
allowance une allocation
allowed permis
almost presque
alone seul
along le long de
Alps les Alpes (f)
already déjà
also, so aussi
always toujours
amazing incroyable
ambition une ambition
ambulance une ambulance
America l'Amérique (f)
American américain
amidst au milieu de, parmi
amount la quantité
amusing amusant, drôle
angry fâché, en colère; **to get angry** se mettre en colère
animal un animal, une bête
ankle la cheville
annoyed ennuyé
annoying ennuyeux (-euse)
anorak un anorak
anxious inquiet (-ète); **to be anxious** s'inquiéter
anything else? et avec ça?
apart from à part
to **apologize** s'excuser
to **appear** sembler, paraître, apparaître
appetising appétissant
apple la pomme

to **apply** (*for a job*) poser sa candidature
to **appreciate** apprécier
to **approach** approcher, s'approcher (de)
to **approve of** approuver
apricot un abricot
April avril
area (*place*) un endroit; (*part of town*) un quartier; (*part of country*) une région
around autour (de); **all around** tout autour
arrival une arrivée
to **arrive** arriver
as, like comme
ashamed: to be ashamed avoir honte
ashtray le cendrier
aside, on one side à part
to **ask** (**for**) demander
aspirin l'aspirine (f)
to **assure** assurer
athletic sportif (-ive)
Atlantic (**Ocean**) l'Atlantique (m)
atmosphere une ambiance
attack, fit la crise
attendant: petrol attendant le pompiste
August août
aunt la tante
automatic automatique
autumn l'automne (m); **in autumn** en automne
avenue une avenue
away: 10 km away à 10 km; **a long way away** loin
awful affreux (-euse), moche, terrible

baby le bébé
bachelor le célibataire

back le dos; *(rear)* l'arrière *(m)*; **to be back** être de retour

bad mauvais; **too bad!** tant pis!

badly mal

bag le sac

baker le boulanger

baker's la boulangerie

balance le solde

balcony le balcon

ball le ballon, la balle

ballet le ballet

banana la banane

bandage, plaster le pansement

bank la banque

bank note le billet de banque

banking: banking transactions opérations bancaires

bar le bar

Barclaycard, Visa card la carte bleue

barmaid la serveuse

basement le sous-sol

bath le bain, la baignoire; **to have a bath** prendre un bain

to **bathe** se baigner

bathroom la salle de bains

baths, swimming pool la piscine

battery la batterie, la pile

to **be** être, se trouver

beach la plage

bean le haricot; **green bean** le haricot vert

beard la barbe

beautiful beau, belle

because parce que, car; **because of** à cause de

to **become** devenir

bed le lit; **to go to bed** se coucher; **to stay in bed** garder le lit

bedroom la chambre

beef le boeuf

beer la bière

before avant (de)

to **begin** commencer; **to begin again** recommencer

beginning le début; **at the**

beginning of au début de

behind derrière; en arrière

Belgian belge

to **belong** appartenir

below en bas

belt la ceinture; **safety belt** la ceinture de sécurité

bend *(in road)* le virage

bicyle le vélo, la bicyclette; **by bicycle** à (en) vélo

bidet le bidet

big, tall grand; **big, fat** gros (grosse)

bill la note, l'addition *(f)*

biology la biologie

bird un oiseau

birth la naissance

birthday un anniversaire; **happy birthday!** bon anniversaire!

biro le stylo (-bille)

biscuit le biscuit

black noir

blanket la couverture

block *(of flats)* un immeuble

blood le sang

blouse le chemisier

blue bleu

board: full board la pension complète; **half board** la demi-pension

boat le bateau; **by boat** en bateau, par le bateau

bomber jacket le blouson

to **book, reserve** réserver, retenir

book le livre

booking, reservation la réservation

booklet le carnet (for tickets, addresses, cheques)

boot *(of car)* le coffre; *(footwear)* la botte

booth: telephone booth la cabine téléphonique

bored: to be bored s'ennuyer

boring ennuyeux (-euse)

born né(e); **to be born** naître

to **borrow** emprunter

boss le patron, la patronne

bother! zut!

bottle la bouteille

boulevard le boulevard

bowl le bol

box la boîte; **telephone box** la cabine téléphonique; **letter-box** la boîte aux lettres

boy le garçon

to **brake** freiner

brake le frein

bread le pain, la baguette

to **break** casser; **to break one's arm** se casser le bras

break *(between lessons)* la récréation

to **break down** être en panne, tomber en panne

breakdown *(mechanical)* la panne; *(detailed account)* le décompte

breakfast le petit déjeuner

bridge le pont

briefs le slip, la culotte

to **bring** apporter

Britain la Grande-Bretagne

Brittany la Bretagne

British britannique

broadcast *(TV or radio)* une émission

broken down en panne

brother le frère

brown brun, marron *(m & f)*

to **brush** brosser

Brussels Bruxelles

budget le budget

buffet le buffet

building le bâtiment

bulb une ampoule

bureau: information bureau le syndicat d'initiative, S.I.

to **burgle** cambrioler

to **burn** brûler; **to burn one's hand** se brûler la main

burst *(tyre)* crevé

bus un autobus, un bus; **by bus** en bus, en autobus; **bus stop** un arrêt

business les affaires *(f)*; *(commercial enterprise)* le commerce; **business man/woman** homme/

femme d'affaires

business course les cours commerciaux (*m*)

busy: to be busy doing sth s'occuper à faire qch

but mais

butcher le boucher, le charcutier

butcher's la boucherie, la charcuterie

butter le beurre

button le bouton

to **buy** acheter

by par

cabbage le chou

cake le gâteau; **cake shop** la pâtisserie

calf le veau

to **call** appeler; **to be called** s'appeler; **to call back** rappeler; **to make a reverse-charge call** téléphoner en PCV; **who's calling?** c'est de la part de qui?

call (*on phone*) le coup de téléphone

calm calme

calor gas le butane; **calor gas store** le dépôt de butane

camera un appareil (-photo)

to **camp** camper

campsite le camping, le terrain de camping

camper le campeur

camping le camping; **to go camping** faire du camping

Canada le Canada; **in/to Canada** au Canada

Canadian canadien

canteen la cantine

capable capable

car une auto, une voiture; **car park** le parking; **'cars for hire'** 'location de voitures'

carafe la carafe

caravan la caravane

card la carte; **banker's card** la carte bancaire; **credit card** la carte de crédit

cards: to play cards jouer aux cartes

career la carrière

careful: be careful! attention!; **to be careful** faire attention

careless impudent, négligent; (*of work*) peu soigné

caretaker le/la concierge

carriage la voiture

to **carry** porter

cartoon le dessin animé

case la valise

case: in that case en ce cas, dans ce cas

to **cash a cheque** toucher/ encaisser un chèque

cash l'argent (*m*)

cashdesk la caisse

cassette la cassette; **cassette recorder** le magnétophone (à cassettes)

castle le château

cat le chat

cathedral la cathédrale

cauliflower le chou-fleur

cellar la cave

centime le centime

centimetre le centimètre

centre le centre; **town centre** le centre ville; **shopping centre** le centre commercial

century le siècle

certain certain, sûr

certainly certainement, bien sûr

certificate le brevet, le certificat, le diplôme

chair la chaise

champion le champion

championship le championnat

to **change** changer

change la monnaie

channel (*on TV*) la chaîne; (**English**) **Channel** la Manche

character le caractère

to **charge** (*for*) compter; **to be in charge of** s'occuper de

charge le prix; **excess charge** le supplément

charming charmant

cheap bon marché

cheaper moins cher (chère)

to **check** vérifier

check-out la caisse

cheerful gai

cheers! à la tienne/vôtre!

cheese le fromage

chemist le pharmacien

chemist's la pharmacie

cheque le chèque; **traveller's cheque** le chèque de voyage; **cheque made out in the name of** chèque libellé au nom de

cheque book le carnet de chèques

chemistry la chimie

chicken le poulet

child un(e) enfant

chips les frites (*f*)

chocolate le chocolat

choice le choix

to **choose** choisir

Christmas Noël (*m*); **Merry Christmas!** joyeux Noël!

church une église

cider le cidre

cigarette la cigarette

cine-camera la caméra

cinema le cinéma

to **circulate** circuler

class (*at school*) le cours

class la classe; **first class** première classe; **second class** seconde classe; **a second-class ticket** une seconde

classical classique

to **clean** nettoyer; **to have something cleaned** faire nettoyer

clean propre

to **clear** débarrasser (*la table*)

clerk un employé

clinic la clinique

clock une horloge

to **close** fermer

closed fermé

clothes les vêtements (*m*)

club le club; **youth club** la maison des jeunes

clutch un embrayage
coach (*bus*) un (auto)car; **by coach** en (auto)car; (*rail*) le wagon, la voiture
coast la côte
coat le manteau
coca-cola le coca
coffee le café; (*white*) le café-crème, le café au lait
coffee pot la cafetière
coin la pièce
cold froid; **to have a cold** avoir un rhume, être enrhumé
colleague le/la collègue
collection la collection; (*of post*) la levée
to **collide with** entrer en collision avec, heurter
collision la collision
colour la couleur; **what colour?** de quelle couleur?
to **come** venir; **to come back** revenir
comedian le comédien, la comédienne
comfort le confort
comfortable confortable
commercial commercial, commerçant
compartment le compartiment
to **complain** se plaindre (de qch), faire une réclamation (contre qn)
complaint la réclamation
complete complet
completely complètement
compliment le compliment
compulsory obligatoire
computer un ordinateur
concert le concert
condition (*state*) un état; **in good/bad condition** en bon/mauvais état
conductor (*on bus*) le receveur
confident ferme
to **congratulate** féliciter
congratulations les compliments (*m*); **congratulations!** félicitations!

connection (*in metro*) la correspondance
consulate le consulat
consulting room la salle de consultation
to **contact** contacter
to **continue** continuer
contraption le machin
convenient commode
conversion un aménagement
converted aménagé
to **cook** faire la cuisine
cook le chef
cooked cuit; **well cooked** bien cuit
cooker la cuisinière
corner le coin
to **correct** corriger
correct exact, correct
to **cost** coûter
cotton le coton; **made of cotton** en coton; **cotton wool** le coton hydrophile
couchette la couchette
council flat un HLM
couch le canapé
to **cough** tousser
counter (*in bank, post office*) le guichet; (*in shop*) le rayon, le comptoir
country le pays
countryside la campagne
course le cours
cousin le cousin, la cousine
cover charge le couvert
cow la vache
cream la crème
credit le crédit
cricket le cricket
crisps les chips (*m*)
critical critique
to **criticize** critiquer
croissant le croissant
to **cross** traverser
crossroads le carrefour
to **cry** pleurer
cup la tasse
to **cure** guérir
currency (*foreign*) les devises étrangères (*f*)
customs la douane; **customs duty** la taxe
to **cut** couper

cycling le cyclisme
cyclist le/la cycliste

daily quotidien (-enne)
dairy la crémerie
danger le danger
dangerous dangereux (-euse)
to **dance** danser
dance le bal
to **dare** oser
dark foncé
date la date
daughter la fille
day le jour, la journée; **the next day** le lendemain; **the day before** la veille; **the day before yesterday** avant-hier; **the day after tomorrow** après-demain
dead mort
to **deal with** s'occuper de
dear cher (chère)
December décembre
to **decide** décider
to **declare** déclarer; **nothing to declare** rien à déclarer
decorator le décorateur, la décoratrice
deep profond
delay le retard
delicatessen la charcuterie
delicious délicieux (-euse)
delighted ravi, enchanté
dentist le/la dentiste
deodorant le déodorant
department le département
departure le départ
to **depend** dépendre; **that depends** ça dépend
to **deposit** déposer
deposit les arrhes (*fpl*)
to **describe** décrire
description la description
desk (*cashdesk*) la caisse
dessert le dessert
destination la destination
to **detest** détester, avoir horreur (de)
to **dial** composer le numéro; **to dial 999** appeler police-secours

dialling tone la tonalité
diarrhoea la diarrhée
to **die** mourir
diesel (oil) le gas-oil
difference la différence
different différent
difficult difficile
to **dine** dîner
dining-room la salle à manger
diploma le brevet, le certificat, le diplôme
direction le sens, la direction; **all directions** toutes directions
dirty sale
disappointed déçu
to **disapprove of** désapprouver
disco la disco(thèque)
to **discuss** discuter
disgusting dégoûtant
dish le plat
displeased mécontent
distance la distance
distant loin, éloigné
distressed désolé, malheureux (-euse)
to **disturb** déranger
diversion la déviation
divorced divorcé
to **DIY** faire du bricolage
DIY le bricolage
to **do** faire; **to do the housework/shopping/washing-up** faire le ménage/les courses/la vaisselle
doctor le docteur, le médecin
documentary le documentaire
dog le chien
door la porte, la portière
dormitory le dortoir
dozen la douzaine
to **doubt** douter
doubt le doute; **no doubt** sans doute
Dover Douvres
drawing le dessin
dress la robe
to **drink** boire
drink la boisson

drinkable (*of water*) potable; **(non-) drinking water** eau (non) potable
to **drive** conduire, rouler
drive la randonnée
drives le chauffeur, le conducteur
to **drown** (se) noyer
drunk ivre
dry-cleaning le nettoyage à sec
dubbed in French en version française
duration la durée
during pendant
dust la poussière
dustbin la poubelle
Dutch hollandais

each chaque; **each person/day/night** par personne/jour/nuit; **one franc each** F1 la pièce
each (one) chacun(e)
ear une oreille
early de bonne heure
to **earn, win** gagner
east l'est (*m*)
Easter Pâques
easy facile
to **eat** manger
to **economise** économiser
edge le bord
Edinburgh Edimbourg
education l'enseignement (*m*), l'éducation (*f*)
effort: it's not worth the effort ce n'est pas la peine
egg un oeuf
elbow le coude
elder aîné
electric électrique
electrician un électricien
electricity l'électricité (*f*)
elegant élégant
emergency exit la sortie de secours
employee un employé, une employée
employer un employeur
empty vide
end la fin, le bout; **at the end of** au bout de

engaged (*number, seat, toilet*) occupé; (*taxi*) pris, pas libre; (*bethrothed*) fiancé
engagement les fiançailles (*f*)
engine le moteur
England l'Angleterre (*f*)
English anglais
to **enjoy oneself** s'amuser
enjoy your meal! bon appétit!
enough assez; **that's enough** ça suffit!
to **enrol** s'inscrire
entertainment la distraction
entirely entièrement, complètement, tout à fait, totalement
entrance une entrée
envelope une enveloppe
equal égal
error une erreur
escalator un escalier roulant (-elle)
essential essentiel (-elle)
Europe l'Europe (*f*)
European européen
even même
evening le soir, la soirée; **in the evening** le soir, en soirée; **good evening!** bonsoir!
everybody tout le monde
everywhere partout
exact juste, exact
exactly exactement
to **exaggerate** exagérer
exam un examen; **to take an exam** passer un examen
example un exemple
excellent excellent
except (for) sauf, à part, à l'exception de
excess fare le supplément
to **exchange** échanger, changer
exchange un échange
exchange bureau le bureau de change
exchange rate (at today's price) le cours du change (au cours du jour)
excuse une excuse
excuse me! excusez-moi, pardon!

to **exist** exister
exit la sortie; **emergency exit** la sortie de secours
expenditure la dépense
expenses les frais (m)
expensive cher (chère); **not very expensive** pas très cher; **not too expensive** pas trop cher
to **explain** expliquer
extra en plus, supplémentaire
extraordinary extra-ordinaire
extremely extrêmement
eye un oeil (pl yeux)

face le visage, la figure
face flannel le gant de toilette
facing en face de, faisant face à
factory une usine
to **fail** (an exam) coller
to **faint** (s')évanouir
fair (hair) blond
false faux (fausse)
family la famille; (adj) familial
famous célèbre
far (from) loin (de); **as far as** jusqu'à
fare stage la section
farm la ferme
fascinating passionnant
fashion la mode
fashionable à la mode
father le père; **father-in-law** le beau-père
fault la faute; (flaw) le défaut
favourite préféré
feast (day) la fête; **happy feast day!** bonne fête!
February février
fed up: to be fed up with it en avoir marre, en avoir assez
to **feel** (se) sentir
ferry le ferry; **by ferry** en ferry
fiancé(e) le fiancé, la fiancée
field le champ
to **fill (in)** remplir; **to fill up**

with petrol faire le plein
film (in cinema) le film; (for camera) la pellicule; **comedy/detective/horror/love film** le film comique/policier/d'épouvante/d'amour
finally enfin, finalement
to **find** trouver; **to find again** retrouver
fine une amende
finger le doigt
to **finish** finir
fire! au feu!
fireman le (sapeur-)pompier
firm ferme, solide
first premier (-ère); **first of all** d'abord
fish le poisson
fishing la pêche
fitted out aménagé
to **fix** fixer, arranger, réparer
flash le flash
flat un appartement
flats (block of) un immeuble
flavour le parfum
flight le vol
floor (storey) un étage; (boards) le plancher, le parquet; **ground floor** le rez-de-chaussée; **on the floor** par terre
flower la fleur
'flu la grippe
fluently couramment
to **fly** voler
fog le brouillard
to **follow** suivre
food les provisions (f); **seafood** les fruits de mer (m)
foot le pied; **on foot** à pied
football le football
footpath le sentier, le chemin
for pour; (because) car
forbidden interdit, défendu; **...is forbidden** défense de ...
foreign étranger (-ère)
forest la forêt
to **forget** oublier
to **forgive** pardonner, excuser; **forgive me** excusez-moi

fork la fourchette
form la fiche, le bon; **order form** le bon de commande
formerly autrefois
formula le formulaire
fragile fragile
franc le franc
France la France
frankly franchement
free libre; gratuit
freezer le congélateur
French français
to **frequent** fréquenter
Friday vendredi
friend un(e) ami(e), un(e) camarade, un(e) copin(e)
from du, de la, des; **(starting) from** à partir de; **originating from** en provenance de
front: in front of devant
frontier la frontière
fruit le fruit; **fruit juice** le jus de fruit
fruiterer le marchand de fruits
frying pan la poêle
full plein; (no vacancies) complet (complète)
fun: to have fun s'amuser
funny amusant, drôle
furious furieux (-euse)
furnished meublé
furnishing l'ameublement (m)
future l'avenir (m)

game le jeu; **games room** la salle de jeux
garage le garage
garden le jardin
gas le gaz
gear la vitesse
general général
generally généralement, en général
gentle doux (-ce)
gentleman le monsieur (pl messieurs)
gently doucement
geography la géographie
German allemand
Germany l'Allemagne (f)

to **get on together** s'entendre
girl la jeune fille
to **give** donner; **to give back** rendre
glass le verre; **to raise one's glass, toast** lever son verre
glasses les lunettes (f)
to **go** aller
to **go and fetch, go for** aller chercher
to **go and see** aller voir
to **go around with** fréquenter
to **go away** s'en aller
to **go camping** faire du camping
to **go down** descendre
to **go home** rentrer
to **go in** entrer
to **go out** sortir
to **go up** monter
to **go with** accompagner
goal le but
good bon(ne); (at a subject) fort
goodbye au revoir
goodness! tiens! mon Dieu!
gramme le gramme
grandchild le petit-enfant (pl petits-enfants)
granddaughter la petite-fille
grandfather le grand-père
grandmother la grand-mère
grandparent le grand-parent
grandson le petit-fils
grape le raisin
grass l'herbe (f)
great! chouette! formidable! sensass! super! épatant! merveilleux!
Great Britain la Grande-Bretagne
green vert
greengrocer le marchand de légumes
grey gris
grocer un épicier
grocer's une alimentation, une épicerie
ground le terrain; **on the ground** par terre

ground floor le rez-de-chaussée
group le groupe
to **guarantee** garantir
guarantee le bon de garantie
guide le guide, le Michelin rouge
guitar la guitare
gymnastics la gymnastique

hair les cheveux (m)
hairdresser le coiffeur, la coiffeuse
half demi; la moitié
hall le vestibule; **town hall** un hôtel de ville
ham le jambon
hand la main
handbag le sac à main
handkerchief le mouchoir
handsome beau (belle)
handy commode
to **hang up** accrocher; (phone) raccrocher
to **happen** se passer, arriver
happy heureux (-euse)
hard dur
hardly à peine
hat le chapeau
to **hate** avoir horreur de
to **have** avoir
to **have to** devoir
head la tête
head teacher le directeur, la directrice
health la santé; **good health!** à la tienne/vôtre! à ta/votre santé!
to **hear** entendre
heart le coeur
heat la chaleur
heatwave la vague de chaleur
heavy lourd
hello! bonjour! (on the phone) allô! **say hello for me** dis/dites-lui bonjour de ma part
to **help** aider, donner un coup de main à
help! au secours!
here ici

here is, here are voici
hi! salut!
high haut
highway code le code de la route
hike la randonnée
to **hire** louer; **hiring** la location
historical historique
history l'histoire (f)
to **hitchhike** faire de l'autostop
hobby le passe-temps, le hobby
hockey le hockey
hole le trou
hold the line! ne quittez pas!
holiday (vacation) les vacances (f); (day off) un (jour de) congé; (public holiday) un jour férié
Holland la Hollande, les Pays-Bas (m)
homework le(s) devoir(s)
honest honnête
to **hope** espérer
horse le cheval
hospital un hôpital
hospitality l'hospitalité (f)
hostess une hôtesse; **air hostess** une hôtesse de l'air
hot chaud
hotel un hôtel
hour une heure
house la maison, le domicile; **at my house** chez moi; **at your house** chez toi/vous
household le ménage
housework le ménage
hovercraft un aéroglisseur
how comment; **how do I get to . . . ?** pour aller à . . . ? **how long?** combien de temps? **how much?** combien? **how much is it?** c'est combien?
however cependant
hunger la faim; **I'm hungry** j'ai faim
hungry: to be hungry avoir faim

to **hurry** se dépêcher
to **hurt** faire mal; **to hurt oneself** se faire mal
hurt blessé
husband le mari
hypermarket un hypermarché

ice la glace
ice-cream la glace
idea une idée
identification la pièce d'identité
identity une identité
if si
ill malade; **to fall ill** tomber malade
illness la maladie
immediately immédiate-ment, tout de suite
important important
impossible impossible
in dans, en
included compris
inclusive compris
incredible incroyable
industrial industriel (-elle)
industry une industrie
to **inform** informer
information les renseignements (*m*)
information bureau le bureau de renseignements, le syndicat d'initiative
inhabitant un habitant
injection la piqûre; **to give an injection** faire une piqûre; **to have an injection** se faire faire une piqûre
insect un insecte
inside dedans
instead of au lieu de
instrument un instrument
to **insult** insulter
insurance l'assurance (*f*)
insured assuré
intelligent intelligent
to **intend** avoir l'intention (de)
intention une intention
to **interest** intéresser; **to take an interest in** s'intéresser à

interesting intéressant
interval un entracte
intolerable inadmissible
to **introduce** présenter; **may I introduce** je te/vous présente
invitation une invitation
to **invite** inviter
Ireland l'Irlande (*f*); **Northern Ireland** l'Irlande du Nord
Irish irlandais
island une île
isn't it? n'est-ce pas?
issue (*of tickets*) la délivrance
Italian italien (-ienne)

jacket la veste, le blouson
jam la confiture
January janvier
jar le pot
jeans le jean
job un emploi, un métier
jobless au chômage
joiner le menuisier
joke la plaisanterie
journey le voyage; **have a good journey!** bon voyage!
jug le pichet, la carafe
July juillet
jumper le tricot, le pull
June juin

to **keep** garder
key la clé (clef)
to **kill** tuer
kilo le kilo
kind aimable
king le roi
to **kiss** embrasser
kitchen la cuisine
knife le couteau
knob le bouton
to **knock down/ over** renverser
to **know** (*a person*) connaître; (*a fact*) savoir

laboratory le laboratoire
ladder une échelle

lady la dame
lake le lac
lamb un agneau
lamp la lampe
language la langue
large grand
to **last** durer
last dernier (-ère); **at last** enfin
late tard, en retard
later tout à l'heure, plus tard
to **laugh** rire
launderette la laverie automatique
lavatory le WC, le cabinet de toilette
lazy paresseux (-euse)
leaflet le dépliant
to **lean** se pencher
to **learn** apprendre
leather le cuir; **made of leather** en cuir
to **leave** quitter, partir (de)
lecture le cours; (*at university*) la conférence
left gauche; **on the left** à gauche
leg la jambe
leisure le loisir; **leisure-time activities** les loisirs (*m*)
lemon le citron
lemonade la limonade
to **lend** prêter
length (*of time*) la durée
less moins; **a little less** un peu moins
to **let** laisser
letter la lettre
letter box la boîte aux lettres
lettuce la salade
library la bibliothèque
licence: driving licence le permis de conduire
life la vie
to **lift the receiver** décrocher (le combiné)
lift un ascenseur
to **light** allumer
light (*weight*) léger (légère); (*colour*) clair
light la lumière, la lampe; **traffic light** le

feu; **red light** le feu rouge
lighter le briquet
to **like** aimer; **I'd like** je
  voudrais; **to like better**
  aimer mieux
lilo le matelas pneumatique
line la ligne
list la liste
to **listen (to)** écouter
litre le litre
little petit; **a little** un peu
to **live** demeurer, habiter,
  vivre, résider
to **lock** fermer à clé (clef)
London Londres
long long (longue); **a long
  time** longtemps
to **look (at)** regarder; **to look
  for** chercher
lorry le camion; **heavy
  goods vehicle** le poids
  lourd
to **lose** perdre
lost: to get lost se perdre
lot: a lot (of) beaucoup (de)
love l'amour (*m*); **in
  love** amoureux (-euse)
lovely beau (belle), ravissant
lozenge la pastille
luck la chance; **good luck!**
  bonne chance!
luckily heureusement
luggage les bagages (*m*);
  luggage rack le filet;
  left-luggage locker la
  consigne automatique
lunch le déjeuner
luxury (*adj*) de (grand) luxe

machine la machine;
  washing machine la
  machine à laver
mad fou (folle)
Madam Madame
magazine le magazine, la
  revue; **weekly magazine**
  un hebdomadaire
mail le courrier
maintenance l'entretien
to **make** faire
  make-up le maquillage
  man un homme

to **manage** se débrouiller
manager le directeur
map la carte; **road map** la
  carte routière
March mars
to **mark** marquer
marks les notes (*f*)
market le marché
married marié
to **marry** épouser, se marier
  avec
match une allumette;
  football match le match
  de football
material (*fabric*) une étoffe
maths les maths, les
  mathématiques (*f*)
**matter: what's the
  matter?** qu'est-ce qu'il y
  a? **it doesn't matter**
  n'importe (où, qui, *etc*)
May mai
mayonnaise la mayonnaise
mayor le maire
meal le repas; **cooked
  meal** le plat cuisiné;
  ready-cooked meal le
  repas préparé; **enjoy your
  meal** bon appétit!
to **mean** vouloir dire; **I mean**
  c'est à dire, je veux dire
means le moyen; **by means
  of** au moyen de
meat la viande
mechanic le/la mécanicien
  (-ne); **garage mechanic/
  owner** le garagiste
medicine la médecine, le
  médicament, le remède
Mediterranean Sea la
  Méditerranée
medium cooked (*of meat*) à
  point
to **meet** (se) rencontrer; faire la
  connaissance de; **meet
  (again)** rejoindre
meeting la conférence, la
  réunion, le rendez-vous;
  **to arrange a meeting
  with s.o.** prendre rendez-
  vous avec qn
melon le melon
member le/la membre
to **mend** raccommoder, réparer

menu la carte, le menu
to **mess up** déranger
metal le métal; **made of
  metal** en métal, de métal
method le moyen
midday midi
middle le milieu; **in the
  middle (of)** au milieu (de)
midnight minuit
milk le lait
million le million
to **mind: I don't mind** ça
  m'est égal
mineral water l'eau
  minérale
minute la minute
to **miss** manquer
Miss Mademoiselle
mistake une erreur; **to be
  mistaken** se tromper,
  faire erreur
**mod. cons.: flat with all
  mod. cons.** un appartement tout confort, de grand
  confort
modern moderne
moment un instant, un
  moment
Monday lundi
money l'argent (*m*);
  pocket money l'argent de
  poche
month le mois
monument le monument
moon la lune
moonlight le clair de lune
moped la mobylette
more plus; **a little
  more** un peu plus
morning le matin, la
  matinée; **in the morning**
  le matin, dans la matinée
most of la plupart de; **at
  the most** au plus
motorbike la moto; **light
  motorbike** le vélomoteur;
  by motorbike à (en)
  moto, á (en) vélomoteur
motorcyclist le motocycliste
mother la mère; **mother-
  in-law** la belle-mère
motorway une autoroute
mountain la montagne
mouth la bouche

to **move** bouger
to **move house** déménager
to **move off** (*vehicle*) démarrer
much beaucoup; **how much?** combien?
municipal municipal
museum le musée
mushroom le champignon
music la musique
musician le musicien
mustard la moutarde

name le nom; **Christian name** le prénom
narrow étroit
national national
natural naturel (-elle)
naturally naturellement
near près de, proche
necessary nécessaire; **it is necessary** il faut
necklace le collier
to **need** avoir besoin de **I need** il me faut
neighbour le/la voisine
neither non plus
nephew le neveu
net (price) net (nette)
never mind! tant pis!
new nouveau (-elle), neuf (neuve); **brand new** tout neuf
news les informations (*f*); les actualités (*f*)
newspaper le journal
next (to) à côté (de); **next** (*in order*) prochain
nice gentil (-ille), aimable, chouette, sympa(thique)
niece la nièce
night la nuit; **good-night!** bonne nuit!
nil zéro
no non; pas (de)
noise le bruit
noisy bruyant
none ne . . . aucun
noon midi
normal normal
normally normalement
Normandy la Normandie
north le nord; **North Sea** la Mer du Nord

nose le nez
not pas (de)
not at all pas du tout; (*in reply to thanks*) de rien, pas de quoi, je vous en prie
note le billet (de dix francs, *etc*); (*invoice*) le bordereau
to **note down** inscrire
to **notice** remarquer
nought zéro
November novembre
now maintenant
number le numéro, le nombre
nurse un infirmier/une infirmière
nursing home la clinique
nylon: made of nylon en nylon

oblong rectangulaire
occasionally de temps en temps
occupied occupé
October octobre
offence (*against the law*) une infraction
to **offer** offrir
office le bureau; **foreign exchange office** le bureau de change; **lost property office** le bureau des objets trouvés; **ticket office** le guichet
officer (*when addressing a policeman*) Monsieur l'agent
often souvent
oil l'huile (*f*)
OK d'accord, entendu; **it's OK** ça va
old ancien (-enne), vieux (vieille), âgé
omelette une omelette
on sur
once une fois, autrefois
one-way sens unique
onion un oignon
only (*adj*) unique; (*adv*) seulement
to **open** ouvrir
open ouvert
opera un opéra

operation une opération
operator un opérateur, une opératrice
opinion un avis, une opinion; **in my opinion** à mon avis
opposite le contraire
opposite (*prep*) en face (de)
optician un opticien
optimistic optimiste
or ou
orange une orange
orangeade une orangeade, une orangina
orchestra un orchestre
to **order** commander
original original; **in the original language** en version originale
other autre
out of order en panne
outside dehors
over par-dessus; **over here** par ici; **over there** par là
overcoat le pardessus
to **overtake** dépasser
owner le propriétaire; (*of café*) le patron

pain: to have a pain (in) avoir mal (à)
pair la paire
pamphlet la brochure
pancake la crêpe
pants le slip, la culotte
paper le papier; **writing paper** le papier à lettres; **(news)paper** le journal
papers les papiers (*m*)
parcel le colis, le paquet
parent le parent
to **park** stationner, (se) garer
park le parc, le jardin public; **car-park** le parking, le stationnement
part: spare part la pièce de rechange
part-time à temps partiel
party la surprise-partie, la boum
to **pass** passer
passer-by le passant

passport le passeport
pastille la pastille
pastries la pâtisserie
pâté le pâté
path le chemin, le sentier
patient le/la patient(e);
(*adj*) patient
pavement le trottoir
to **pay** payer, compter; **to pay
by the word** payer au mot
to **pay back** rembourser
paying (*not free*) payant
payment le règlement, le
paiement
peaceful paisible
peach la pêche
pear la poire
peas les pois (*m*); **garden
peas** les petits pois
pedestrian le piéton;
pedestrian crossing le
passage clouté
pencil le crayon
pen-friend le/la
correspondant(e)
people les gens (*m*); **a lot
of people** beaucoup de
monde
pepper le poivre
per par; **per day/person/
night** par jour/personne/
nuit
perfect parfait
performance la séance
perhaps peut-être
perfume le parfum
perfumery la parfumerie
permanent permanent
permission la permission
person la personne; **per
person** par personne
pessimistic pessimiste
petrol l'essence (*f*); **2/3-
star** l'ordinaire (*m*); **4/5-
star** le super
petrol attendant le/la
pompiste
to **phone** téléphoner, donner
un coup de téléphone,
passer un coup de fil
photo la photo
physics la physique
piano le piano
picnic le pique-nique

picturesque pittoresque
piece le morceau
pig le cochon
pill la pilule
pilot le pilote
pineapple un ananas
pitch le terrain
pity: it's a pity c'est
dommage
to **place** poser, placer
place un endroit, un lieu,
une place; **to take place**
avoir lieu
to **plan** arranger, prévoir
plan le plan
plane un avion; **by plane**
en avion, par avion
plant la plante
plaster le sparadrap
plastic plastique; **made of
plastic** en plastique, de
plastique
plate une assiette
platform le quai, la voie
to **play** jouer; **to play
football** jouer au football;
to play music jouer de la
musique; **to play the
piano** jouer du piano
play la pièce de théâtre
player le joueur
pleasant agréable
to **please** plaire
please s'il te (vous) plaît
pleased content
pleasure le plaisir; **with
pleasure** avec plaisir!
plug la prise (de courant)
plum la prune
plumber le plombier
pocket la poche
to **point out** indiquer
police la police, la
gendarmerie; **police
station** le commissariat, le
poste de police, la
gendarmerie; **police
van** le car de police
policeman un agent de
police, un gendarme
policewoman la femme-
agent de police
policy (*life insurance*) la
police d'assurance

polite poli
poor pauvre; (*at a subject*)
faible
pop (music) le pop
pork le porc
port le port
porter le porteur
possible possible
to **post** mettre à la poste, poster
post la poste, le courrier;
post office le bureau de
poste, les PTT
postbox la boîte aux lettres
postcard la carte postale
postcode le code postal
poster une affiche
postman le facteur
potato la pomme de terre
pound la livre; **pound
sterling** la livre sterling
practical pratique
to **prefer** préférer, aimer mieux
to **prepare** préparer
prescription une
ordonnance
present le cadeau; (*adj*)
présent
to **press** appuyer
pressure la pression
pretty joli
to **prevent** empêcher
price le prix; **maximum
price** le prix maximum;
minimum price le prix
minimum; **price list** le
tarif
priority (*to vehicles on the
right*) priorité à droite;
(*over secondary roads*)
passage protégé; **to have
priority** avoir la priorité,
avoir le droit de passage
private privé
private hospital la clinique
problem le problème; **no
problem!** pas de
problème!
profession le métier, la
profession
programme le programme;
(*on TV*) une émission
progress le progrès
to **promise** promettre
to **pronounce** prononcer

property (*lost*) les objets trouvés
to **protest** protester
proud fier (fière)
to **prove** prouver
public publique
publicity la publicité
pudding le dessert
to **pull** tirer
pullover le pull(over)
to **punch (ticket)** composter
punctual exact
punctured crevé
pungent piquant
to **punish** punir
pupil un(e) élève
purchase un achat
purse le porte-monnaie
to **push** pousser
to **put** mettre, poser;
   to put a question poser une question
pyjamas un pyjama
Pyrenees les Pyrénées (*f*)

quantity la quantité
quarter (*numerical*) le quart; (*area*) le quartier
quay le quai
Quebec Québec
queen la reine
question la question
quickly vite, rapidement;
   too quickly trop vite
quiet calme; **to be quiet** se taire

rabbit le lapin
radiator le radiateur
radio la radio
railway le chemin de fer;
   French Railway la SNCF
to **rain** pleuvoir
raincoat un imperméable
rare rare; (*of meat*) saignant
rarely rarement
raspberry la framboise
rate (*of exchange*) le taux (d'échange)
rather (*instead*) plutôt; (*enough*) assez
razor le rasoir

to **read** lire
ready prêt
really vraiment
rear l'arrière (*m*)
reason la raison
receipt le reçu
to **receive** recevoir
reception la réception
receptionist la réceptionniste
to **reckon** compter
to **recognize** reconnaître
to **recommend** recommander, conseiller
record le disque
record player le tourne-disque, la platine
recreation la distraction; (*at school*) la récréation, la récré
red rouge; (*of hair*) roux (rousse)
reduction la réduction
redundant licencié, au chômage; **to be made redundant** être mis au chômage, être mis à la porte, être licencié(e)
to **refuse** refuser
region la région
to **register** enregistrer
to **regret** regretter
regulations le règlement
to **remain** rester, demeurer
to **remember** se souvenir de, se rappeler
to **rent** louer; **renting** la location
rent le loyer
to **repair** réparer; **to have something repaired** faire réparer
repair la réparation
to **repay** rembourser
to **repeat** répéter; (*a year at school*) doubler
to **replace** remplacer
to **reply** répondre
reply la réponse
report le rapport; (*on an accident*) le constat
to **reserve** réserver
to **respect** respecter
responsible responsable

to **rest** se reposer
rest (*remainder*) le reste
restaurant le restaurant
result le résultat
to **return** retourner
return (*ticket*) un aller-retour
reward la récompense
Rhine le Rhin
rich riche
ride la randonnée
right: to have the right avoir le droit; **to be right** avoir raison
right (*adj*) droit; **on the right** à droite; **just right** à point
to **ring** sonner; (*phone*) un coup de fil/de téléphone
ring un anneau; (*with stone*) une bague
ripe mûr; **nicely ripe** à point
rise une augmentation
risk le risque
road la route, le chemin; **trunk road** la route nationale, la grande route
roadway la chaussée
roadworks les travaux (*m*)
roast rôti
room la salle; **classroom** la salle de classe; **games room** la salle de jeux; **waiting-room** la salle d'attente; (*space*) la place
rope la corde
round autour (de); **all around** tout autour; (*adj*) rond
route un itinéraire; **bus route** la ligne d'autobus
rucksack le sac à dos
rugby le rugby
rules le règlement
to **run** courir
to **run over** renverser, écraser
Russian russe

sad triste
salad(s) les crudités (*f*)
salary le salaire
sales les soldes (*f*); **in a sale** en solde

salesman/woman le vendeur/la vendeuse
salt le sel
salty salé
same même, pareil **all the same** quand même, tout de même
sand le sable
sandal la sandale
sandwich le sandwich
sardine la sardine
satisfied satisfait
Saturday samedi
saucer la soucoupe
sausage le saucisson
to **save up** faire des économies
savings les économies (*f*)
to **say** dire
scene la vue
school une école, un collège, un lycée
science la science
scooter (*motor*) le scooter; **by scooter** en scooter
Scotland l'Ecosse (*f*)
Scottish écossais
sea la mer
seafood les fruits (*m*) de mer
seasick: to be seasick (airsick) (carsick) avoir le mal de mer (de l'air) (de la route)
seasickness le mal de mer
seated assis
second (*in order*) deuxième
secondary secondaire
second-class ticket une seconde
secretary le (la) secrétaire
to **see (one another)** (se) voir; **see you!** à tout à l'heure! **see you on Saturday!** à samedi!
to **seem** sembler, paraître, avoir l'air
self-service store le libre-service
to **sell** vendre
to **send** envoyer
sentence la phrase
separated séparé
separately à part, séparément

September septembre
series (*TV or newspaper*) le feuilleton
serious grave, sérieux (-euse)
seriously gravement, sérieusement
to **serve** servir; **serve/help yourself!** servez-vous!
service le service; **service (not) included** service (non) compris
to **set off** partir
several plusieurs
sex le sexe
shaky: to feel shaky se sentir fragile
shampoo le shampooing
shape la forme
shelf (*in shop*) le rayon
sheep le mouton
sheet le drap; (*paper*) la feuille
shirt la chemise
shoe la chaussure; **shoe repairer's** la cordonnerie
to **shop, go shopping** faire les courses
shop la boutique, le magasin
shopkeeper le commerçant
short court; **short of money** à court d'argent
shorts le short
to **shout** crier
to **show** montrer
show le spectacle; **film show** la séance de cinéma
shower la douche, (*of rain*) une averse; **to have a shower** prendre une douche
shower block le bloc sanitaire
shy timide
sick malade
side la côte
sight la vue
to **sign** signer
signature la signature
silence le silence
since depuis; (*because*) puisque
to **sing** chanter
singer le chanteur, la chanteuse

single (ticket) un aller simple
sink un évier, un bac à vaisselle
Sir Monsieur (*pl* Messieurs)
sister la soeur
to **sit down** s'asseoir; **sit down!** asseyez-vous!
site un emplacement, un site
situated situé
situation la situation
size la taille; (*for shoes, gloves*) la pointure
skiing le ski
skirt la jupe
to **sleep** dormir; **sleep well!** dormez bien!
sleeping bag le sac de couchage
slice la tranche
slim mince
slip (*of paper*) une fiche
slot la fente
slow lent
to **slow down** ralentir
slowly lentement
small petit
smart chic
smell une odeur
smile le sourire
to **smoke** fumer; **(no-) smoking** (non-)fumeur
so (*therefore*) ainsi, donc; (*to such an extent*) tellement
soap le savon
society la société
sock la chaussette
socket la prise (de courant)
some quelques; **someone** quelqu'un; **something** quelque chose
sometimes quelquefois, parfois
somewhere quelque part
son le fils
song la chanson
soon bientôt; **see you soon!** à bientôt!
sorry! pardon! excusez-moi! **to be sorry** regretter, s'excuser; **I'm sorry** je m'excuse, je suis désolé
sort la sorte; **a sort of** une sorte de

Sound and Light (*spectacle*) Son et Lumière
soup le potage, la soupe
south le sud
souvenir le souvenir
space la place; l'espace (*m*)
Spain l'Espagne (*m*)
Spanish espagnol
to **speak** parler
speaking: Paul speaking (*on phone*) Paul à l'appareil; **who's speaking?** c'est de la part de qui?
speciality la spécialité
spectacles les lunettes (*f*)
to **spell** épeler
to **spend** (*time*) passer; (*money*) dépenser
spicy piquant
in **spite of** malgré
spoon la cuiller; **coffee spoon** la cuiller à café
spoonful la cuillerée
sport le sport; **winter sports** les sports d'hiver
spouse un époux, une épouse
to **sprain** (*one's ankle*) se fouler (la cheville)
spring le printemps; **in spring** au printemps
spying l'espionnage (*m*)
square la place; (*adj*) carré
stadium le stade
staircase un escalier
stamp le timbre; **a one-franc stamp** un timbre à un franc
star (*of film*) la vedette
start (*of term, year*) la rentrée
state un état
to **stay** rester
stay le séjour
steady égal, continu, ferme, solide
steak le steak, le biftek; **steak and chips** le steak-frites
stepfather le beau-père
stomach l'estomac (*m*), le ventre
to **stop** arrêter, s'arrêter
store le dépôt

stove le poêle; **oil (paraffin) stove** le poêle à mazout (à pétrole)
strange bizarre
stranger un inconnu
strawberry la fraise
street la rue
string la ficelle
strong fort
student un(e) étudiant(e)
studies les études (*f*)
studio un atelier
to **study** étudier
sturdy solide
subject la matière
subscription la cotisation
sub-title le sous-titre
suburbs la banlieue
to **succeed** réussir
suddenly soudain, tout à coup
to **suffer** souffrir
sugar le sucre
to **suggest** suggérer, proposer
summer l'été (*m*); **in summer** en été
Sunday dimanche
sunny ensoleillé
sunstroke une insolation, un coup de soleil
supermarket le super-marché
supplement le supplément
supplementary supplémentaire
to **suppose** supposer
sure sûr
to **surprise** étonner, surprendre
surprise la surprise
surprising étonnant, surprenant
sweater le tricot, le pull
to **sweep** balayer
sweet le bonbon
sweet doux (douce); **sweetened** sucré
to **swim** nager
swimming la natation
swimsuit le maillot de bain
Swiss suisse
switch l'interrupteur (*m*)
to **switch off** éteindre
Switzerland la Suisse

syllabus le programme
sympathy la sympathie
syrup le sirop; **cough mixture** le sirop contre la toux

table la table
tablet le cachet, le comprimé
to **take** prendre; **to take part (in)** participer (à)
take-away à emporter
tank (*petrol*) le réservoir
tap le robinet, la prise d'eau
tart la tarte
taste le goût
tax la taxe
taxi le taxi; **by taxi** en taxi
tea le thé; **teapot** la théière
teacher (*primary*) un instituteur/une institutrice; (*secondary*) le/la professeur; **headteacher** le directeur, la directrice; (*head of lycée*) le proviseur
team une équipe
teenager un(e) adolescent(e)
to **telephone** téléphoner
telephone le téléphone; **t. directory** un annuaire; **t. box** la cabine téléphonique; **a t. call** un coup de téléphone, un coup de fil
television la télévision, la télé
to **tell** dire; (*narrate*) raconter
temperature la température, la fièvre; **to have a t.** avoir de la température
temporary temporaire
tennis le tennis; **to play tennis** jouer au tennis
tent la tente
term le trimestre
terrific formidable
Thames la Tamise
to **thank** remercier; **thank you very much** merci bien/beaucoup
thanks to grâce à
that ça, cela; **that comes to . . .** ça fait . . .

that way par là
theatre le théâtre
then alors, puis
therefore donc
there y, là; **there is, there are** il y a, voilà; **there you are!** voilà! **there will be** il y aura
thing la chose
thing le machin, le truc
to **think** penser, croire
thirst la soif
thirsty: to be thirsty avoir soif
this ceci
this way par ici
thousand mille
throat la gorge
Thursday jeudi
ticket le billet, le ticket; **ticket office** le guichet; **ticket inspector** (*railway*) le contrôleur
to **tidy** ranger
tidy en ordre
tie la cravate
tights le collant
till la caisse
time le temps, la fois; **from time to time** de temps en temps; **on time** à temps; **a long time** longtemps; **to have the time** avoir le temps; **at what time?** à quelle heure?
timetable un horaire, un emploi du temps
tin (*of food*) la boîte (de conserve); **tin-opener** un ouvre-boîte
tip le pourboire
tired fatigué
title le titre
tobacco le tabac
tobacconist's le bureau de tabac, le café tabac, le tabac
today aujourd'hui; **today's special** le plat du jour
together ensemble
toilet la toilette, le cabinet, le WC
token le jeton
toll (gate) le péage
tomato la tomate

tomorrow demain; **see you tomorrow!** à demain!
too (much) trop; **too bad!** tant pis!
tooth la dent; **toothbrush** la brosse à dents; **toothpaste** la pâte dentifrice, le dentifrice; **to clean one's teeth** se brosser les dents
torch la lampe électrique
torn déchiré
total le montant, le total, la somme
tourism le tourisme
towards vers
towel la serviette; **hand-towel** un essuie-mains; **tea-towel** le torchon
town la ville
toy le jouet
trade le commerce; (*profession*) la profession
traffic light le feu
train le train; **express train** un rapide; **fast train** un express; **high-speed train** un TGV; **non-stop/through train** un train direct; **stopping train** un omnibus; **by train** par le train, en train
transfer le virement; **to make a credit transfer** faire un virement
to **translate** traduire
to **travel** voyager
tray le plateau
tree un arbre
trip une excursion
trouble la peine; **it's not worth the trouble** ce n'est pas la peine
trousers le pantalon
trout la truite
true vrai
to **try** essayer
tube (*of pills*) le tube; (*the Underground*) le métro; **to go by tube** prendre le métro
Tuesday mardi

to **turn** tourner
TV la télé; **TV news** le télé-journal
twice deux fois
two-stroke (engine) le deux-temps
typical typique
typist le/la dactylo
tyre le pneu
twin un jumeau/une jumelle

ugly laid, moche, vilain
umbrella le parapluie
unbearable insupportable
uncle un oncle
underdone saignant
Underground le métro; **by Underground** en métro
underneath sous, au-dessous de, (en) dessous
to **understand** comprendre
underwear les sous-vêtements (*m*)
undressed déshabillé; **to get undressed** se déshabiller
undrinkable (*of water*) non potable
unemployed en chômage; **unemployed person** le chômeur, la chômeuse
unemployment le chômage
unfortunately malheur-eusement; **unfortunately not!** hélas non!
unhappy malheureux (-euse)
union le syndicat; **union member** le syndiqué
United Kingdom le Royaume-Uni
United States les Etats-Unis (*m*)
university une université
unwell souffrant
upkeep l'entretien (*m*)
urgent urgent
to **use** utiliser; **to use sparingly** économiser
useful utile
usherette une ouvreuse

useless inutile
usual normal
usually généralement,
d'habitude, en général

vanilla la vanille
varied varié
vegetable le légume
vehicle la voiture, le
véhicule
very très
view la vue
village le village
violin le violon
to **visit** visiter, rendre visite
à; **just visiting** de
passage à
visit la visite
visitor le visiteur, la
visiteuse
voice la voix
to **vomit** vomir

wage le salaire, la paie
wage-earner le(la)
salarié(e)
waist la taille
to **wait (for)** attendre
waiter le garçon (de café), le
serveur
waitress la serveuse
to **wake** (se) réveiller
Wales le Pays de Galles
to **walk** marcher, se
promener; **to go for a
walk** faire une promenade
walk la promenade, la
randonnée
wall le mur
wallet le portefeuille
wallpaper le papier peint
to **want** vouloir, désirer, avoir
envie de
war la guerre
warden le gardien; **with
resident warden** gardé
to **warn** avertir
to **wash** (se) laver; **to wash
up** faire la vaisselle
wash (*e.g. car wash*) le lavage

washbasin le lavabo
washroom les toilettes (*f*)
watch la montre
water l'eau (*f*); **water
supply point** la prise
d'eau
to **wear** porter
weather le temps
wedding la noce, les noces
Wednesday mercredi
week la semaine
weekend le week-end
to **weigh** peser
welcome bienvenu; **you're
welcome!** (*in reply to
thanks*) de rien!
well bien; (*exclamation*) eh
bien! **well done!** bravo!
quite well pas mal
Welsh gallois
west l'ouest (*m*)
western (*film*) le western
wet mouillé
what quoi, qu'est-ce que
wheel la roue; **spare
wheel** la roue de secours
when quand
where où
which quel(le); **which
(one)** lequel (laquelle); **of
which** dont
white blanc (blanche)
who qui; **who's speaking?**
c'est de la part de qui?
whose dont
why pourquoi
wide large
widow la veuve
widower le veuf
wife la femme
willing: I'm quite willing
je veux bien
willingly volontiers
window la fenêtre; **shop
window** la vitrine
to **win** gagner
wine le vin (blanc, rouge,
rose, *etc*)
winter l'hiver (*m*); **in
winter** en hiver
to **wipe** essuyer
to **wish** vouloir; **to wish good**

luck souhaiter bonne
chance
with avec
without sans
witness le témoin
woman la femme
wood le bois; **made of
wood** en bois
wool la laine
word le mot; **in other
words** autrement dit
to **work** travailler; (*to be in
working order*) marcher;
it's not working ça ne
marche pas
work le travail; **manual
work** les travaux manuels
worker un ouvrier, une
ouvrière
workshop un atelier
world le monde
worn (-out) usé
to **worry** s'inquiéter
worth: it's worth ça vaut
wrist le poignet
to **write** écrire
writing paper le papier à
lettres
wrong: to be wrong avoir
tort

yard la cour
year un an, une année; **all
year** toute l'année;
happy New Year! bonne
année!
yellow jaune
yesterday hier
yet pourtant
yoghourt le yaourt
young jeune; **youngest
child** le cadet, la cadette
youth la jeunesse
youth hostel une auberge
de jeunesse

zero zéro
zone la zone
zoo le jardin zoologique, le
zoo